The Spectre at the Feast

Also by Andrew Gamble

The Conservative Nation
Britain in Decline
The Free Economy and the Strong State
Hayek: The Iron Cage of Liberty
Politics and Fate
Between Europe and America

The Spectre at the Feast

Capitalist Crisis and the Politics of Recession

Andrew Gamble

First published 2009 by
PALGRAVE MACMILLAN

Palgrave Macmillan in the UK is an imprint of Macmillan Publishers Limited, registered in England, company number 785998, of Houndmills, Basingstoke, Hampshire RG21 6XS.

Palgrave Macmillan in the US is a division of St Martin's Press LLC, 175 Fifth Avenue, New York, NY 10010.

Palgrave Macmillan is the global academic imprint of the above companies and has companies and representatives throughout the world.

Palgrave® and Macmillan® are registered trademarks in the United States, the United Kingdom, Europe and other countries.

ISBN-13: 978–0–230–23074–3   hardback
ISBN-10: 0–230–23074–1   hardback
ISBN-13: 978–0–230–23075–0   paperback
ISBN-10: 0–230–23075–X   paperback

This book is printed on paper suitable for recycling and made from fully managed and sustained forest sources. Logging, pulping and manufacturing processes are expected to conform to the environmental regulations of the country of origin.

A catalogue record for this book is available from the British Library.

A catalog record for this book is available from the Library of Congress.

10 9 8 7 6 5 4 3 2 1
18 17 16 15 14 13 12 11 10 09

Printed and bound in Great Britain by
CPI Antony Rowe, Chippenham and Eastbourne

In memory of **Malcolm Bowie**

The road to excess leads to the palace of wisdom. For we never know what is enough until we know what is more than enough.
William Blake

Like one that on a lonesome road
Doth walk in fear and dread,
And having once turned round walks on,
And turns no more his head;
Because he knows a frightful fiend
Doth close behind him tread.
Samuel Coleridge

Contents

List of Tables and Figures

Tables

Figures

Preface

The subject of this short book is the extraordinary series of events which have taken place in the world economy and world politics since the summer of 2007. The book seeks to provide some ways of understanding their origins and possible consequences, by relating them to their wider intellectual and historical context, and reflecting on their significance. The crisis is far from over, and events are fast moving. There will be many books written about them in the future, and no one treatment can hope to be definitive. This book is about the politics of the crisis, how it arose, how we might understand it, what are its consequences, how far it might go and what might be done.

The book does not carry references in the text except for direct quotations, but I have added a guide to reading, which indicates some of my main sources, and hopefully this will be more useful to the reader than the conventional kind of references. An earlier version of some sections of Chapter 3 first appeared in a chapter of a book edited by Richard Robison, *The Neo-Liberal Revolution: Forging the Market State* (Palgrave Macmillan, 2006).

The idea for this book came from my publisher Steven Kennedy, who has given me great support and advice during the writing of it. Wyn Grant and another reviewer gave me extremely valuable comments on a first draft. I have tried to incorporate their comments and criticisms into the final text. This book draws on many years of discussion of these themes with friends and colleagues, and I am very grateful to them and also for invitations to present some of the ideas contained here at recent seminars and conferences in Warwick, Belfast, Brussels and Cambridge. Sarah Gamble provided some very useful research assistance.

I have learned a great deal about different perspectives in politics and political economy in the last ten years by being involved in the editing of two journals *The Political Quarterly* and *New Political Economy*, and I have also benefited greatly from discussions with my students at Sheffield and at Cambridge. Writing books is a lonely occupation, and not really to be recommended, but hopefully this book will stimulate some debate and prompt further reflection on what has become one of the most important issues of our time.

Queens' College, Cambridge   ANDREW GAMBLE

Introduction: The Road to Excess

For fifteen years after the end of the Cold War between the Soviet Union and the West in 1991 the rich countries of the capitalist West enjoyed a remarkable feast. Fuelled by ever-higher levels of personal and corporate debt and by the abundance of cheap manufactures from rising economic powers such as India and China, the consumers of the rich countries went shopping. Like bubbles breaking through the surface of a volcanic swamp, swelling and swelling until they burst, so asset bubbles regularly formed in the financial markets, in shares, in housing and in certain commodities such as oil. The two great bubbles of the period between 1992 and 2008 were the bubble in shares, which ended in the dot.com slump in 2000, and the bubble in housing, which ended in the credit crunch in 2007–8. When the housing bubble collapsed, the American satirical magazine *The Onion* demanded that the American people be given another bubble to invest in.

Prices of assets caught in a bubble soared, while saving ratios plummeted. More and more individuals were sucked into the spending spree. Conspicuous consumption, once the badge of the leisure class, was now engaged in by all but the poorest. Spending and borrowing escalated, and consumers, whatever their income and their ability to pay, were bombarded with offers to take out more loans and accept more credit cards. Alan Greenspan, Chairman of the Federal Reserve between 1987 and 2006, marvelled at the 'irrational exuberance' of the markets, but did little to curb it. Everyone assumed each bubble could be managed and burst at the right time by appropriate action by the authorities. What few people recognized was that the activities of finance had transformed the entire economy into one giant bubble, and no-one was calculating the risks of what would happen if that burst.

The boom first got under way in the 1980s, but was then interrupted. It resumed in earnest in the 1990s, and came to a decisive end in 2008. It spread its benefits unevenly, as all booms do, but these benefits were considerable, and it bears comparison with spectacular booms of the past, including the 'Great Prosperity', the long boom in the 1950s and 1960s after the Second World War, and the 'Roaring Twenties', the boom partic-

1

ularly in the United States after the First World War. The origins of this latest boom lay in decisions taken by US administrations in the 1970s and 1980s, which changed the role of the United States in the global economy, ended the period of high inflation, high unemployment and slow economic growth in the 1970s, and made possible the ascendancy of finance to a position of dominance it had not enjoyed for sixty years, since before the onset of the Great Depression in the 1930s. The dominance of finance and the financial markets at the end of the twentieth century was seen by many observers, including Susan Strange, Herman Schwartz, Peter Gowan and Andrew Glyn, as greater in certain respects than at any previous time in the history of capitalism. It is hardly surprising that, as in previous booms, the same illusions came to prevail. At the height of the boom it seemed possible, against all historical experience to the contrary, that this time it might really last for ever. The era of boom and bust had finally passed away, and the global economy was now so sophisticated, so flexible, so interdependent, that its breakdown was now unthinkable. It performed miracles of coordination every day, and the fact that no-one properly understood how they were accomplished only added to the marvel and the mystery. It was widely perceived, however, that these miracles would not be possible without the financial markets. The masters of these markets came to be revered as the architects of prosperity. When Alan Greenspan received an honorary knighthood from the Queen of England in 2002 the citation spoke of his services to economic stability.

Economic progress had not been uninterrupted and smooth during his tenure. There were ups and downs, financial alarms, even recessions. Some countries experienced severe financial and growth problems. There was a major global downturn in 1990–2, and the start of a deep financial crisis in Japan, which caused the Japanese economy to stagnate through the 1990s. In 1997 many of the economies of East and South East Asia were caught up in a severe financial crisis. There were scares in the United States also, notably the bursting of the dot.com boom in 2000 and the earlier collapse of a major hedge fund, Long Term Capital Management (LTCM) in 1997. LTCM had been highly successful investing a portfolio of $125 billion on behalf of its clients. Using mathematical models devised by two Nobel Laureates, Robert Merton and Myron Scholes, it borrowed more than $120 billion on the financial markets to fund high-risk deals, and built up $125 trillion in financial derivatives, contracts with other financial institutions, much of it off balance sheet. At the time of its collapse, the firm had borrowed more than $35 dollars for every dollar it owned. This was leveraging on a grand scale, and a portent of things to come. Once it suffered a major default LTCM was overwhelmed and could not meet its liabilities. But in 1997 it was an isolated case, and few heeded the lesson. The New York Fed stepped in to limit the damage, and persuaded a number of major Wall Street banks to take the hedge fund over and absorb its losses. Many of the other financial storms that blew up proved local or regional in their effects, and did not spread to the whole system. Particularly in the heartland of the global economy, the United States, problems that emerged were successfully managed. Most of the diners barely noticed when some of the guests had to be carried out.

The feast has been marked by excess and exuberance, summed up for many in the jubilant faces of City traders celebrating their annual and increasingly extravagant bonuses. But by no means everyone has had a seat at the table. Like the animals at the conclusion of *Animal Farm*, many have been left to peer in through the windows, watching their masters eat. But for those that have been seated, the urge to consume in ever-greater quantities, and to finance it by taking on more and more debt, has been extremely strong. Many warnings were issued, but few restraints were successfully applied. During the upswing there was a rush into assets and commodities and away from cash, as the various bubbles inflated, giving huge paper profits to individuals and companies on their houses and investments. In ten years, in many leading economies house prices increased by more than 75 per cent in real terms, and in some countries, including Britain, Australia and Spain, they more than doubled. In Ireland they almost trebled. An increasing part of the money fuelling the surge in prices was speculative, based on the calculation that the market could only go up, and that housing as an investment offered some of the highest returns on the market.

In its later stages, the feast was maintained by many individuals choosing to sustain their spending by borrowing, taking the risk that the market would still carry on going up. But another of its features was the explosion of rewards for those on the top table. The old habit of partnerships in the City of London distributing annually the profits of the business among the partners, who typically did not take a salary, was transformed on Wall Street in the 1980s and 1990s into the bonus culture, where investment bankers and corporate executives began to be paid bonuses that were not linked directly to performance or results, and were colossal in absolute terms. Even banks that had to be bailed out in 2008 were so locked into these habits that they still planned to distribute huge bonuses to their senior executives, until the Obama administration in January 2009 expressly forbade it. The class of super-rich expanded considerably in the 1990s. Many of them contrived to pay no taxes in the country in which they lived. The amount of money held offshore in tax havens rocketed. Huge salaries became the norm for many different types of celebrities, media presenters, sports stars and movie actors, as well as bankers. The result was ostentation and material indulgence on a grand scale. The era of capitalist excess, which had been so marked at the beginning of the twentieth century, was back.

The series of events that began in 2007 struck like an earthquake at the heart of the institutions, practices and beliefs of the last twenty-five years, and the aftershocks will be felt for a long time. These events became popularly known as the credit crunch, although it quickly became clear that much more than a credit crunch was involved. It began in the United States, but spread to other leading economies, and has since engulfed the whole world. It has conjured up an old spectre, the spectre of economic and political collapse and of a general crisis of capitalism, which many thought had been finally exorcised. A temporary financial crash, followed by a normal recession would be painful but manageable. There have been many in the past. A crisis of capitalism would signal a much more far-reaching political and economic impasse, manifested in unpredictable and sometimes uncontrollable events, and which at the extreme threatens slump, depression, polarization, political unrest, even war, affecting all parts of the global economy and the international state system.

After the credit crunch began in the summer of 2007, the world's financial and political leaders gradually became aware of the enormous risks to stability that it was unleashing. Increasingly frantic efforts have been made to stave off disaster, and ensure that, at the very least, the more malign features of past crises of capitalism are not repeated. During 2008 this became the focus of concern. Certainly the appearance of this spectre at the feast, like Banquo's ghost, has given little time to think of anything else. Those in charge of the feast think, like Macbeth, that they can banish it and then resume their places and carry on as before. But the longer the crisis has lasted the less likely that appears. This feast is over.

It is not the only spectre stalking the planet. Other even more threatening spectres loom over us, the spectres of climate change and nuclear war, which threaten not just the economic well-being but the continued existence of the human species. The spectre of capitalist crisis may currently absorb our attention, and lead us to avert our gaze from these other spectres, but they have not gone away, as Furio Cerutti has recently reminded us. The interruption to the feast, if it is prolonged enough, will not start to reverse the damage that climate change is doing, only moderate the rate at which the damage is being inflicted. If the feast is resumed at some point on the old basis, all advantage will be quickly lost. All three problems will have to be tackled if the human species is to have a future, and this means the feast cannot be allowed to continue on the old basis, even if it proved possible to do so. Any serious way forward has to secure international cooperation on all three of these major complex problems, however daunting that may seem, when political agreement on even the simplest issues is so hard.

To understand what is happening we must first focus on the causes and consequences of the financial crash, which began with a few small tremors in 2007 and gradually erupted into something on a scale which was beyond any recent experience. By the end of 2008 it was clear that this was the most serious financial crash since 1929. Whatever happens in the next few years, 2008 will be remembered as one of the most dramatic and extraordinary financial crashes in the history of capitalism. But a financial crash is not the same as a crisis of capitalism. It may signal one, and they have often been intimately connected in the past, but not always. There are examples of financial crashes which were just self-contained events, and did not trigger any wider consequences. During the boom itself there were several moments in the dizzy ascent of the markets which it was thought at the time might be the turning point, the moment when the market decisively turned down, but which in the end proved not to be.

By the beginning of 2009 there were many signs that the financial crash of 2008 was becoming a wider crisis, with the onset of a major global recession, no end in sight to the problems of the banking system, growing fears of a new protectionism in trade and finance threatening to put globalization into reverse, and increasing social and political unrest in many countries. Events are fast moving, and this book does not try to make predictions about what will happen next, but to provide a guide to key issues and ideas, and the wider context in which these events should be understood. It asks whether the crisis could have been prevented, what are its possible consequences, how far it might go, how profound it may turn out to be, and what the main ideas being canvassed for dealing with it are. It offers a number of ways of thinking about the crisis and its impact; historical, political and economic. It examines how far this crash is similar to past financial crashes, and how far it is new, and what the likely consequences are if it becomes a more general capitalist crisis. The political economy of the crisis in this broad sense is the main focus of the book.

Financial crashes are endemic to capitalism. Despite the optimism often expressed throughout the history of capitalism that such episodes have finally been overcome, and the cycles of boom and bust banished, these hopes have always turned out in the end to be illusory. The way in which financial markets operate in capitalism, as Charles Kindleberger has argued, means that periods of irrational exuberance and financial bubbles which expand until they burst, leading to a financial crash and the taking of emergency financial corrective measures, are not accidental events but should always be expected. The history of such financial crises goes back a very long way. Speculation in 1720 in the stock of the South Sea Company, which had plans to trade with Spain's South American colonies, created one of the most famous bubbles in history, the South Sea Bubble. The Company proposed to exchange half of Britain's national debt for its own shares, and to convert the debt to a lower interest rate. Its share price soared from £128 to £1,000 in eight months. There were, however, no earnings to justify this share price, so once the market's rise faltered, the shares declined precipitately in value and many of the shareholders, particularly those who had borrowed to buy their shares, were ruined.

In the nineteenth century such crashes became a regular feature of the ten-year business cycle which became established in several national economies. Capitalism was, however, still at a very early stage in its development as a global economy, and business cycles were often not synchronized, being determined by local circumstances. The swings in activity from peak to trough were very large, and the impact on those bankrupted and thrown out of work was severe. In the twentieth century the global economy which had emerged by 1914 brought about a new stage in the organization of national economies and a new form of generalized capitalist crisis, discussed in Chapter 2, which contained major moments both of danger and of transformation, involving not just economic but political restructuring, and not just within states but between states. In a major capitalist crisis of this kind the crash that occurs may not only be of stock markets and currencies, of jobs and businesses, but can also involve ideological and political orthodoxies, and international economic arrangements. Such crises are different from ordinary recessions because they are always both political and economic in nature, and they can affect not just individual national economies, but the whole world economy. In the last hundred years there have only been two such crises, the first occurring in the 1930s, which has become known by the name Americans gave to it, the Great Depression, and the second in the 1970s, which lacks an agreed

name, but was characterized by stagflation, the combination of high inflation, high unemployment and stagnant or slow growth. This book argues
that we are entering a third such crisis today.

Much misunderstanding arises because of a failure to distinguish
between different kinds of crisis, the term crisis being thrown around fairly
indiscriminately in everyday discourse. Looked at in terms of their role in
the business cycle, financial crashes have long been seen as a product of
the dynamism and exuberance of this form of economy. They are an essential moment in the process of creative destruction, as Joseph Schumpeter
understood, regularly sweeping away established activities and obstacles
to growth, allowing new initiatives, new opportunities and new technologies to emerge. Such a process requires political underpinning and political intervention. But crises of capitalism go much further. They are
intensely political in nature, and because of that they are unique events.
They follow no particular cyclical pattern, they do not necessarily repeat
the sequences of the past, but they do share some common features, in
particular because they can become the occasion for much more far-reaching political change both within states and between states. They create the
conditions for the rise of new forms of politics and policy regimes, and the
rebalancing of power between states, through war or other means. Their
outcomes have been new institutions, new alignments, new policies, and
new ideologies. They come retrospectively to be seen as major turning
points. The transformations they engineer are generally protracted, and
although they are often associated with dramatic events, there is rarely one
decisive moment.

There is nothing inevitable about the form that crises take, or about their
outcomes. A crisis of capitalism does not mean the end of capitalism, or
even the beginning of the end. It is rather a period when capitalism is reorganized. The financial crashes that regularly punctuated the capitalist business cycle in the nineteenth century did not signal the end of capitalism, as
many socialist critics of capitalism confidently expected, and neither did
the two generalized capitalist crises of the twentieth century prove fatal to
capitalism's survival. Both can be seen in retrospect as creating the conditions for its renewal, and for a further period of expansion. It was not capitalism but socialism which collapsed in the twentieth century, both as a
political movement and as an intellectual alternative to capitalism. Long
before its final downfall as an economic rival to capitalism, Friedrich
Hayek declared triumphantly, 'Surely it is high time for us to cry from the
housetops that the intellectual foundations for socialism have all

collapsed' (Hayek, 1978, p. 305). Shortly before the opening of the Berlin Wall, Francis Fukuyama announced the end of history, and that market capitalism and representative democracy were now the horizon of possibility in the modern world. But such attempts to draw lines in history and award victory to one side or another are likely to seem arbitrary and premature to future generations. Global capitalism in its modern form has existed for less than two centuries. So far, in this short history, despite a turbulent career, it has survived every crisis, whether financial, economic or political, and has emerged strengthened each time. But to imagine that it is therefore immortal displays the same kind of hubris that investment bankers and neo-classical economists were exhaling at the height of the credit boom. Robert Lucas, the chairman of the American Economic Association in 2003, even claimed that the central problem of 'depression-prevention' had been solved, for all practical purposes.

Hubris has not been absent from capitalism's enemies either. Karl Marx and Friedrich Engels opened the *Communist Manifesto*, published in 1848, by proclaiming: 'A spectre is haunting Europe; the spectre of communism', and went on to identify the gravediggers of capitalism, the industrial proletariat, whom they confidently believed would bury it, and hopefully in their lifetime. At times the gravediggers appeared to be massing, but they have never struck. Today, as the capitalist wagon careers out of control down the track, spilling its load and its passengers, there are few gravediggers in sight. Financial crashes may be moments of danger, but they also have been a necessary means by which the conditions for capitalism to continue are renewed, and the foundations for further expansion and growth laid. No two financial crashes are the same. There are some common features, but the context is always different. It would be foolish therefore to attempt to predict the outcome of the current financial crash on the basis of experience of previous ones. It is particularly hard to predict the political responses and the political fallout. What can be done is to establish criteria for judging the scale of the crash that occurred in 2008, the range of possible political responses, and to ask whether it might become a full generalized crisis of the political and economic order, a capitalist crisis in the terminology of this book. Such crises can develop in very different ways, and there is nothing that makes any particular outcome inevitable.

In thinking about the 2008 financial crash and what it might bring in the future, we therefore need to pay attention to the politics of crisis at least as much as to the economics. The politics will be shaped by the economics but will not be determined by it. Particularly when a crisis is of this magnitude, its political aspect is fundamental to understanding its outcomes and its consequences. States have been active in shaping the response to it, and will be crucial for its resolution. A capitalist crisis in the sense in which I am using the term signals major adjustments for particular powers and regimes. Current developments put a special spotlight on the United States. The book will ask whether some of the events we are witnessing – the collapse of a particular growth model and ideology, the discrediting of many of the prescriptions of neo-liberalism, and the dramatic return of the state, in the form of bank bailouts and nationalizations – constitute a permanent and major political and ideological shift, or whether the changes will only prove to be temporary, leading to a restoration of the economic and political order pretty much as it was, once the worst of the downturn is over. Do these events signal the 'return of history', in the sense of the recovery of a real debate about political alternatives and political possibility and a sober assessment of the threats to the survival of the human species, the final laying to rest of the triumphalism which accompanied the fall of communism, and which survived even the shock of 9/11? Or after an interval will it be business as usual again?

A critical question is whether the United States has either the political will or the political means to renew its global leadership. The election of Barack Obama in November 2008 was widely seen as a new beginning, and the determination to take a different course, but whether an Obama presidency has the political capacity to deliver on its promises and to fulfil the expectations it has aroused has yet to be tested. The domestic pressures for the United States to become more isolationist and protectionist will be intense, and the difficulties of finding multilateral solutions severe, in part because to succeed the United States will have to acknowledge its weakened position in the world following this crisis, and act accordingly. The question for the United States is whether to emphasize dominance or leadership. At one time it enjoyed both; now it has to choose. Yet without the United States multilateral solutions to the crisis are unlikely to work, since there is currently no substitute for the United States, and many countries, including the European states, still look to the United States to continue to play a global role, and bear the burdens of leadership which it assumed almost seventy years ago. What is at stake is whether the American world order, which has been reconfigured more than once since 1945, is now due to be reconfigured again, and in ways which might allow a new period of American leadership, or whether the Americans will merely seek to preserve their dominance. In either case, we are entering a new and much more uncertain era where no state is in an automatic position to dominate or to govern the global economy.

The Plan of the Book

This book is an exploration of how crises arise under capitalism and how they may be explained. It takes the view that while there have been many recessions in the last hundred years there have been only two generalized crises of capitalism. These crises take the form of prolonged periods of political, economic and ideological impasse. The first occurred in the 1930s, the second in the 1970s. We may be entering a third. This book suggests that we are. Such crises are, above all, political events; they arise politically, they are constructed politically and they are resolved politically.

Chapter 1 explores the 2008 financial crash and the reasons for it. It looks at how the boom of the 1990s and the bubble economy had their origins in the way the global economy was reconstructed in the 1970s. The solutions for that crisis created the conditions for the next. The chapter explores the sequence of events, which was known at first as the credit crunch, because it was thought to be a problem confined to the financial markets. It was not long, however, before it became recognized as something much more serious. The sequence of events by which the credit crunch turned into a financial crash and then into a global recession is set out.

Chapter 2 asks how we should understand the nature of this downturn. It has already been constructed in media throughout the world as a crisis. But what kind of crisis? Is it a mere hiccup in the triumphal procession of globalization and liberalization which have been sweeping the world in the last three decades? Or does it portend a new generalized capitalist crisis. How can we distinguish between different forms of crisis, and how can we decide how profound any particular crisis is or might become, particularly when we are in the middle of it? What concepts and theories can we draw on to make sense of it? The chapter discusses different meanings of 'crisis', and how these meanings have changed from the views of early capitalism put forward by the classical political economists, including Marx, who treated capitalist crisis as arising inexorably from the laws of political economy. Such an approach was continued in the twentieth century by liberal political economists such as Friedrich Hayek and Joseph Schumpeter and socialist political economists like Ernest Mandel. But there were also much more political conceptions of crisis being developed by Karl Polanyi and later Jurgen Habermas, as well as subtle accounts of the possibilities of political intervention to solve crises associated with John Maynard Keynes and Hyman Minsky. The growth of the state and the new balance of power in the international state system in the twentieth century changed the meaning of capitalist crisis, and altered the political response. It became the responsibility of governments to manage crises and if possible avoid them altogether. This had major consequences for the politics of these crises, and how they were understood. Crises were not natural events outside human control, but were socially constructed, and the way in which they were constructed determined how they were resolved, and in whose interests.

Chapter 3 asks what the consequences of this crisis are for the ideologies and discourses which have dominated the last thirty years, in particular neo-liberalism and globalization. How much will they be discredited by recent events in the financial markets? How damaged is the growth model which they promoted? Will this downturn just be a short interlude before the next stage of neo-liberal globalization, or will new ideologies and discourses emerge? The chapter explores the different strands of globalization and of neo-liberalism, and the many tensions within them. It looks at how neo-liberalism became the dominant common sense, and what its prospects are, whether it can regain its ascendancy by constructing a narrative around this crisis as it did for the last.

Chapter 4 asks what the political consequences of the crash and the ensuing downturn are, particularly for the leading states of Anglo-America, Britain and the United States, which have been at the centre of the liberal world order for so long. It looks at the political fallout of the recession and the implications for incumbent governments and political leaders, comparing it with experience from the two previous major recessions in the 1930s and 1970s. It looks in particular at the impact on the United States, still the global leader and the state which alone is in a position to chart a way out of the crisis for the global economy, and discusses whether it has the capacity and the skill to make the attempt.

Chapter 5 asks what are the consequences of these events are for the global economy and the balance between states. It explores whether one outcome of the crisis will be a major shift in power from the United States to the rising economic powers, or whether the weakness of other states, both established and rising, and the continued strategic strengths of the United States will allow it to preserve its position, reconstruct the governance of the global economy, and launch a new phase of expansion.

Chapter 6 asks could anything have been done to prevent this crisis, and what now needs to be done? It asks how the crisis is likely to develop, and outlines some of the different attempts to set the crisis in context and to provide solutions. It details some of the main arguments associated with market fundamentalists, national protectionists, regulatory liberals, cosmopolitan liberals and anti-capitalists. It concludes by summarizing the main argument of the book.

1
From Boom to Bust

The long economic upswing that culminated in the financial crash of 2008 began in the 1980s in the United States and in the United Kingdom, and was underpinned by a new growth model, which had the financial markets at its core, and the ambition to make every citizen an independent financial subject. This model pinpointed the route out of the stagflation of the 1970s, which eventually was to give rise to a new prosperity and renew the economic ascendancy of the United States. It accompanied and helped make possible a major restructuring of the global economy, involving a shift in many of the leading economies from manufacturing to services, an acceleration of the trends towards globalization, the introduction of new information technologies, the adoption of neo-liberal ideas across the whole field of public policy and a reorganization of the state.

The early signs, however, were not propitious. The major crisis of the 1970s had created deep problems of stagflation, which persisted long into the 1980s. Inflation rose again to over 20 per cent in the UK in 1980 and 13 per cent in the US, and unemployment climbed sharply. In the UK it reached 11 per cent or 3 million by 1982 and stayed there until 1986. In the US it reached 9.7 per cent in 1982. But relief was at hand. The first major upswing of the new era got under way in the second half of the 1980s, particularly after 1986, and both unemployment and inflation fell. This first upswing was to be cut short by the recession of the early 1990s, but although painful this was relatively short-lived, and after 1992 growth resumed in earnest. The boom was under way.

One of the significant changes given credit for laying the foundations of the boom and the financial growth model at its heart were the new doctrines of monetarism and supply-side economics that came to prominence in the 1970s and 1980s, particularly in Anglo-America, and the institutional and policy changes which they helped inspire and for which they provided the rationale. Rebuilding the foundations of sound money after the turmoil of the 1970s was a priority for the Thatcher Government, elected in 1979, and also for the Reagan Administration, elected in 1980. The Thatcher Government pursued a tough monetary and fiscal policy in its early years, which brought down inflation but at the cost of a doubling of unemployment. The political purpose of the government was not just to create monetary stability but also to defeat the special interests in the shape of public sector trade unions and local governments, which constantly threatened to undermine it. A bruising series of conflicts ensued, which eventually created the political conditions in Britain for the introduction of the new supply-side economics. In the US there was a sharp recession at the beginning of the 1980s, as a result of a severe monetary squeeze by the Federal Reserve, but then followed an experiment with supply-side economics, in a bid to return the economy to growth. Some of this was inadvertent. The government slashed taxes but could not get Congressional approval for its spending cuts. It went ahead with the tax cuts anyway and in some areas, particularly the military budget, spending increased. The result was a ballooning deficit, leading to the $3 trillion debt made famous by Ross Perot in his campaign for a balanced budget in the 1992 presidential race. This was only the beginning. By 2007 the US national debt had reached $5 trillion (see Figure 1.1).

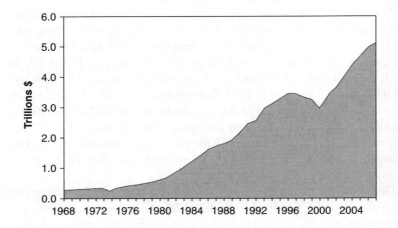

Figure 1.1   The US national debt, 1968–2007

Source: data from US Department of the Treasury, www.treasurydirect.gov

Officially both the Reagan and the Thatcher governments were mone-tarist. But this did not mean that they sought to go back to a pre-Keynesian era in political economy. In one sense both remained fundamentally Keynesian in their policy stance, This was partly because monetarism in the strict technical sense could not be made to work, as the Thatcher Government discovered. Every measure of control of money was quickly subverted by the markets. But it was also because when it came to it there was little political appetite for trying to restore sound money by making the state truly limited, and giving up all the direct and indirect levers that had been developed for influencing the economy. The rhetoric was often anti-Keynesian, but much of the practice fitted neatly within a Keynesian frame-work. But this was Keynesianism with a difference. It was what Colin Crouch has aptly called 'privatized Keynesianism'. This new financial growth model used tax cuts to stimulate the economy, and it promoted priva-tization of public assets and deregulation of the private sector, particularly the financial sector. It sought to expand credit, not restrict it, and to enlist the financial sector as the most important driver of growth and competition in the economy. It led to the rise of the investment banks and the rating agen-cies to their commanding position in the global economy at the beginning of the twenty-first century, and the proliferation of new financial vehicles and instruments, a readiness to 'leverage' every asset whether in the public or private sector, and to make all citizens and organizations 'financial subjects'. Leveraging meant simply using existing assets and income to borrow in order to invest in other assets which promised a higher return. Applied to individuals and companies this meant taking on ever larger burdens of debt, in relation to what they already owned or earned, to be redeemed against future earnings or, in the case of government organizations, taxes. The inge-nuity of the financial sector was set to work to create new ways of spreading risks, new ways of expanding credit, new ways to encourage individuals, companies and governments to borrow, employing new devices such as financial derivatives and credit default swaps, and in this way to keep spend-ing, asset prices and jobs continually rising. The credit rating which individ-uals, companies and governments received became very important in determining the amount of credit they could obtain, and great ingenuity went into devising ways in which high credit ratings could be given to those who would once have been judged to be poor credit risks. In this way credit could continue to expand, drawing in more and more citizens and companies. If it worked everyone could become rich painlessly. As one advertising slogan suggested, it took the waiting out of wanting.

One of the most important conditions for this new financial growth model to become fully established was the deregulation of the financial markets. This had been proceeding steadily for some time, but in the 1980s it was given a major boost. In the UK, the so-called 'Big Bang' of 1986 swept away many of the restrictions, which had determined the kind of banks which could locate in London and how they traded. The City of London had once been the preserve of a relatively small and cohesive financial elite, whose businesses were founded on close personal connections and trust. In throwing open the City to competition, the Thatcher Government was pursuing what it believed to be the right policy for all parts of the economy. Exposure to international competition with no guarantees from the government was tough medicine but considered the best way the City could sustain and develop its international role.

The financial revolution in London and New York in the 1980s was to have profound consequences. The main driver was the US financial sector, and the re-establishment of its global dominance. An important part of its global reach was being able to create a network of other financial centres around the world in which American banks and their subsidiaries could operate freely. This network included Hong Kong, Tokyo, Singapore and London. The traditional willingness of the British to treat the City of London as an 'offshore island' with more freedom to operate independently than most other national financial centres, made London the ideal partner for Wall Street. Within twenty years the financial sector in London had become one of the UK's largest employers and export earners, and in comparative terms was large in relation to the rest of the economy. Some smaller economies, like Iceland and Switzerland, went even further, but among the large economies, none rivalled Britain for the relative size of its financial sector. It accounted for 5 per cent of gross domestic product (GDP) and over a million employees, and gave Britain the largest trade surplus in financial services in the world. (In 2003 it totalled $25.3 billion, more than twice as much again as the next largest surplus, that of Switzerland.) The British government actively encouraged the growth of the financial sector and the service sector more generally to replace the gap left by the decline of manufacturing and the older industrial towns and cities.

Susan Strange called this new financial growth model 'casino capitalism'. It created a rapidly expanding financial sector, which was increasingly separate from the rest of the economy, intensely competitive, fast moving, nimble and innovative, brilliant at calculating margins and exploiting opportunities. Its business was trading in financial claims, and as the boom developed speculation became an ever more important part of its activities. As Keynes remarked in *The General Theory of Employment, Interest and Money*, published in 1936:

> Speculators may do no harm as bubbles on a steady stream of enterprise. But the position is serious when enterprise becomes the bubble on a whirlpool of speculation. When the capital development of a country becomes the by-product of the activities of a casino, the job is likely to be ill-done. (Keynes, 1973, p. 159)

Casino capitalism was to flourish, particularly in what later became known as the Anglosphere economies, consisting of the United States, Canada, Britain, Ireland, Australia and New Zealand, and particularly in the heart of the Anglosphere – the United States and Britain, or Anglo-America. These countries not only shared a common language, but common political and legal traditions, and a form of capitalism noted for its emphasis on flexible labour markets, shareholder value and highly developed financial sectors.

The alternative to casino capitalism in the 1980s was the model of capitalism represented by Germany and Japan, with its emphasis on long-term investment in capacity and skills, the nurturing of successful businesses, life-long relationships with employees and the subordination of finance to those ends. The short-termism in the Anglosphere economies induced by the increasing dependence of companies on the financial markets and by their need to focus relentlessly on increasing shareholder value appeared for a time during the 1980s to make the financial growth model look distinctly inferior to the investment growth model. Japan and Germany were regarded by many as having devised a much more effective and sustainable form of capitalism, which would finally consign the Anglosphere model to the scrapheap, and oblige them to adopt German and Japanese institutions.

That is not what happened. The Japanese economy stalled at the beginning of the 1990s because of the bursting of its own local financial bubble that had been allowed to form in property prices. The uncertain response by the Japanese authorities to this crisis pushed Japan into a deflationary spiral from which it did not properly emerge for ten years. It retained its position as the world's second largest economy, but its growth rate declined sharply, and it no longer looked like an economy that was about to overtake the United States, or that could offer a successful model to the rest of the world. Germany was preoccupied in the 1990s with the absorption of the East German economy following reunification, which proved much more protracted and complex than had been envisaged. German growth slowed, and its attraction as an alternative model sharply decreased. After the end of the recession at the beginning of the 1990s and the extraction of sterling from the European Exchange Rate Mechanism in 1992, the financial growth model of the Anglo-Saxons began to sweep all before it. The European and the Japanese banks became deeply integrated into the complex financial web which was spun in the 1990s. There was still resistance in many countries to accepting the full Anglo-American medicine of flexibility, deregulation, tax cuts and privatization, but the hegemony of Anglo-American finance was not contested. Everyone queued up to join this particular part of the feast.

A second major factor which made the boom possible was the emergence of China, India, Brazil and other rising economic powers in the 1990s. The dramatic leap, in particular, of Chinese economic growth in the 1990s, propelled by the movement of rural workers into the cities on the eastern coastal strip, made possible a supply of cheap manufactured goods which kept inflation low in the rich countries. The high savings ratio in China created large surpluses, which were lent to western governments and western banks, and helped create the credit to allow consumers to continue buying the goods China was producing. The bringing into play of such vast populations in both world production and world trade was a transformative event for the global economy, and helped create the conditions in which the financial growth model could succeed for such a long time, despite the numerous bubbles and instabilities, and the huge imbalances in surpluses and deficits which piled up inexorably. The low inflation and the seemingly endless expansion of credit brought a mood of euphoria to the markets, which after a time seemed to infect the regulators as well.

As the boom developed there were numerous fears expressed that it was unsustainable, and that the build-up of consumer debt and current account deficits, particularly in the United States and the United Kingdom, and the vast surpluses elsewhere which were being used to finance them, would at some stage require a correction. By 2008 there were $3 trillion held in the Sovereign Wealth Funds of China, Saudi Arabia and Russia, a sum higher than the GDP of the United Kingdom, the world's fifth largest economy. Consumer debt in the UK reached £1.44 billion in June 2008, higher than total UK output. Household, banking and corporate debt combined reached 350 per cent of US GDP and 300 per cent of UK GDP. With remarkable prescience, the Pope had declared in 1985 that the foundations of the world economy were unstable and would lead at some point to a collapse. Unfortunately, the warning was rather too general to be of immediate use in the financial markets, and the heavens did not fall. Some academics and some financial journalists warned that the boom could not continue indefinitely, but their advice was not heeded. This was partly because those with very real knowledge and concern about the risks that were being run could always be accused of crying 'wolf' when the crisis did not then materialize, or did not spread. The more knowledgeable critics suffered too from being lumped together with some of those offering 'independent' financial advice. There were a series of financial newsletters in the years running up to the crash with doom-laden predictions of 'Apocalypse Now'. Sooner or later one of them had to be right. Whenever one of the bubbles burst, or was deliberately collapsed, there was an outpouring of dire warnings that this time the end really was nigh. But the markets steadied themselves and growth resumed. Everyone involved in the markets and in regulating the markets had a sense that it was too good to last. But, while it lasted, no-one was inclined to act the sheriff. No-one wanted to turn off the fuel that was powering the boom. No-one wanted to think about the crash.

The Credit Crunch

The boom was powered from many different sources, and there was not one bubble but several. Once the financial growth model got into its stride, it spewed out bubbles. There were bubbles in different kinds of financial assets and in commodities. But the most important bubbles were in dot.com shares, which burst in 2000, and subsequently in housing (see Figure 1.2).

It was the bursting of the housing bubble that brought the whole global financial structure crashing down in 2008 and plunged the world into recession in 2009. The problem began in the US housing market. The federal authorities raised interest rates from 1 per cent in 2004 to 5.35 per cent in 2006, and they went on climbing, peaking at 6 per cent in 2007. This was a steep rise but not unusual. It represented the kind of active monetary policy which all central banks had become used to conducting, aiming to stabilize their economies and keep them growing. The Federal

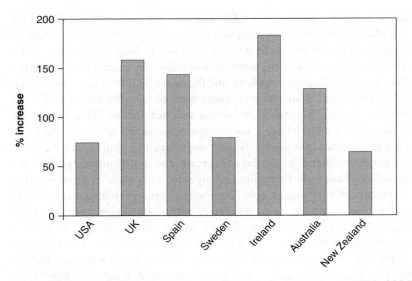

Figure 1.2 Average percentage increases in house prices, 1997–2005 (selected countries)

Source: data from Blyth (2008) from original source Wyss (2007).

Reserve judged that credit conditions were too lax now that the economy had recovered from the mini recession it had suffered in 2001–2, after the bursting of the dot.com bubble, and that credit should become tighter to reduce the risk of inflation. This meant restricting the flow of credit in key areas like housing. This was a normal operation, which had been performed many times before. It had the desired result. The squeeze on credit made house prices start to fall, as the supply of new mortgages dried up and some of those with mortgages were forced to default. This too had happened many times before and in itself was no cause for alarm. It was part of the normal housing cycle. A period of greater tightness in the market, and a downward adjustment of prices would be followed by the return of buyers to the market, as credit became more freely available again, and prices would resume their upward march.

This time was different. The number of homeowners defaulting rose to record levels in 2006 and 2007 in the US. Those defaulting most heavily were those who had sub-prime loans. The term 'sub-prime' is one of those masterly circumlocutions which litter the English language. Calling loans 'sub-prime' is like calling execution 'termination with extreme prejudice'. Sub-prime loans were developed by the financial services industry to keep the housing boom going. They involved making high-risk loans to applicants with poor or non-existent credit histories, people who would be classed as very poor risks in normal circumstances and shut out of the market. There was something egalitarian and inclusive about sub-prime loans. Their origins lay in the 1970s, in the Community Reinvestment Act passed in 1977 under the Carter administration. It imposed an obligation on banks to provide mortgages to low-income families, and listed a number of criteria and a number of compliance measures. It had some powerful political supporters in Congress, because it was seen as a way of at last reaching into the ghettos and extending homeownership to that minority of the population that had never previously enjoyed it. The legislation worked well, but in 1997 there was a significant change. Bear Stearns, the investment bank, created the first securitization of Community Reinvestment Act loans, which were guaranteed by Freddie Mac, one of the leading US mortgage lenders, and given the top triple A credit rating. These securities were soon many times oversubscribed. The mistake, however, was not the policy of trying to get low-income families on the housing ladder, but putting investment banks in charge of delivering it. They came up with an ingenious solution which achieved a key public policy goal at minimal cost to the public purse, by distributing the costs elsewhere. The consequences were largely unforeseen.

The problem with sub-prime loans was that the people taking out these loans were in no position to afford them once interest rates rose sharply as they did after 2004, as part of a general monetary correction, and there were no arrangements in place to cushion them against such changes. In ordinary times this would have had serious consequences for a large number of borrowers who could no longer meet the repayments on their loans. But it would not have had wider implications for the whole financial system. The reason that it did in 2007 was the inverted pyramid which the financial services industry had created on the back of sub-prime lending. On the strength of the new assets they had acquired the banks proved ingenious at bundling together the loans and securitizing them, turning them into investment bonds which were sold on to other financial interests. In many instances these bonds were triple A rated by the rating agencies of Wall Street, the guardians of financial probity. A triple A rating was conferred on those companies, countries and investment products where the investors could have strong confidence in the soundness of the bonds.

In this case, however, far from being sound the bonds were hollow. There were no secure income streams behind them, and once many mortgagees started to default on their loans, the precariousness of the imposing financial structure, which the financial services industry had created, was exposed. It had been erected on the supposition that sub-prime loans were just, in fact, like any other housing loan. In their search for ever more lucrative income-bearing assets, banks and other financial institutions had invested in the sub-prime market by buying the securitized investment products the financial services had developed. So global and interdependent had the financial system become that banks all around the world had bought these products, boosted their balance sheets and used them as justification for increasing their own lending. One of the most extraordinary features of the credit crunch as it unfolded was the light it threw on the lending practices of banks, and the extent of financial globalization, the way in which banks in Iceland and throughout the European Union had become responsible for sub-prime loans issued in local housing markets in the United States. What became clear was that the banks had no way of independently assessing the value of many of the assets they so freely added to their balance sheets, and which they used to increase their lending. They relied on the judgements of the rating agencies. What the rating agencies were basing their judgements on was unclear.

During the second half of 2007 events began to move at a quickening pace. The chronology of some of the main events through 2007 and 2008 is set out in Table 1.1. Signs that all was not well in the sub-prime market began to multiply in 2007. An American bank, New Century Financial, which specialized in sub-prime mortgages, filed for bankruptcy in April 2007 and reduced its workforce by half. Many of its debts had been taken on by other banks, so the collapse of New Century Financial sent ripples throughout the financial markets. Many other financial institutions were forced to realize that they might have to write off that part of their assets based on sub-prime loans. There were many variations in the way different banks were affected, but those that were most exposed, those that had chosen to make involvement in the sub-prime loan market a major part of their business suddenly found themselves in great peril. The first major name to get in trouble was Bear Stearns, the investment bank, which in July 2007 had to announce a total loss in two of its hedge funds. Those who had invested in them stood to lose all their investment. Bear Stearns had tried hard to avert this outcome, and had tried to raise money from other banks to tide it over. But it failed to persuade other banks to lend to

Table 1.1   Chronology of the crisis, July 2007–February 2009

2007	
July	Bear Stearns announces major losses on hedge funds
August	Severe tightening in wholesale money markets
	Federal Reserve cuts lending rate to 4.75%
September	Run on Northern Rock
Sept–Dec	Federal Reserve cuts lending rate to 4.25%
	Major international banks announce losses
	Credit ratings of bond insurers reduced
December	Federal Reserve announces major loan package to banks
2008	
January	Major falls in stock markets
	House prices start to fall
February	Federal Reserve cuts lending rate to 3%
March	Northern Rock nationalized
April	Bear Stearns taken over by JP Morgan Chase
July	IMF predicts financial losses will be $1 trillion
September	Collapse of IndyMac
	Bail out for Freddie Mac and Fannie Mae
	Collapse of Lehman Brothers
	Merrill Lynch taken over by Bank of America
	HBOS taken over by Lloyds TSB
	Numerous bank rescues, bailouts, nationalizations
	$700 billion bailout rejected by US Congress
October	Wall Street collapse
	Further falls in stock markets
	Further bailouts and rescue packages
	Further reductions in interest rates
	G7 proposes five-point action plan
November	Steve Forbes declares the worst is over
December	European Central Bank reduces lending rate to 3.25%
	IMF announces rescue package for Iceland
	Federal Reserve reduces lending rate to 0–0.25%
	US announces rescue package for Ford, GM and Chrysler
2009	
January	IMF predicts worst recession for advanced economies since 1945
February	Bank of England reduces lending rate to 1%
March	Bank of England reduces interest rate to 0.5%
April	G20 Summit in London

it or to guarantee its sub-prime investments, because by this time other banks had become seriously alarmed by their own exposure to bad debts arising from sub-prime. This was the new element which was to become such an important feature of the next eighteen months. The confidence of banks in one another, and their willingness therefore to lend to one another, and to take over bad debts, had begun to weaken. At the height of the crisis it was to disappear altogether. At the beginning of 2009 it had still not returned.

During July and August 2007, the financial markets became aware that the sub-prime loans which had been such an important source of new income in the previous decade were no longer secure, and that the banks across the world faced major losses. Central banks began to intervene at this point, injecting extra liquidity in a bid to persuade banks to keep lending to one another and to tide the markets over the worst effects of the collapse of the sub-prime market. Ben Bernanke, chairman of the Federal Reserve, warned that the losses involved could run to $100 billion. Compared to what was to come that was to seem a modest sum. It was at this time that the term 'credit crunch' began to be used, to refer both to the increasing difficulties some borrowers were having in securing loans, and to the growing unwillingness of banks to lend to one another, when the reason for the loan was to shore up bad debts. The financial authorities were sufficiently concerned to make the first moves in bringing down interest rates and expanding liquidity. On 17 August, the Fed made the first cut in its lending rate, by 0.5 per cent to 4.75 per cent.

The problems in the banking sector continued to worsen, however, during August 2007, with several other banks which were heavily involved in the sub-prime market in the US or who had engaged in lending to borrowers who were high credit risks within their own national economy getting into difficulties and being forced to default. Sachsen Landesbank, a German regional bank, got into trouble and was taken over by another Landesbank. Across Europe a number of financial institutions began reporting losses from their investments in the US sub-prime market, while in Britain, where sub-prime lending had also flourished, although not to the same extent, and under a different name, banks began cutting back on the loans they were prepared to make.

At this point the situation looked serious but still manageable. What gave the authorities greatest cause for concern in the two leading financial centres, Britain and the United States, was the growing divergence between the interest rate at which the Bank of England and the Federal

Reserve was prepared to lend to the banks and the interest rate at which banks were prepared to lend to one another. In London the key rate was the London Interbank Offered Rate (LIBOR), which had come into existence in 1984 to provide some uniformity to the different interest rates at which banks could borrow unsecured funds from other banks on the London wholesale money markets. Since then these two rates had normally been very close, but in August 2007 they began to diverge markedly. LIBOR rose to 6.79 per cent, while Bank Rate was 5.75 per cent. This was to become one of the hallmarks of the financial crisis. The divergence reflected a breakdown in trust between the banks themselves. They had begun to lose confidence in the ability of other banks to pay back money that was advanced to them, and they wanted to be sure of having the money available for their own needs, so began to demand a premium for making any such payments. This made it much more difficult for banks that got into trouble to borrow from their fellow banks to tide them over. This drying up of liquidity became one of the most visible signs of the growing credit crunch, as banks began to take a hard look at what was on their balance sheets, and which assets were backed by solid income streams. The more they probed, the more they realized that they did not know the full extent of their potential liabilities, and therefore could not estimate the full extent of their exposure to bad debts within the global financial system. The result of thousands of bankers all making individual decisions about their own businesses led cumulatively to a sharp contraction of credit and a collapse in confidence and trust. It created a downward spiral, with assets having to be regularly marked down and value destroyed. The disappearance of so much wealth into a black hole caused perturbation. What the banks had created they were now forced to destroy. The anguished cry from media presenters, 'Where has all the money gone?', suggested that someone must have stolen it. The truth was even more shocking. The values which had been posted as the bubbles inflated had always contained a large element that was fictitious, as market insiders knew only too well. The trick was always to sell up before the market turned. Some called it swimming naked in the ocean. No-one could tell who was naked until the tide went out.

In September 2007 the growing tightness in the financial markets produced a run on a bank, Northern Rock. This was one of the new UK banks which had emerged from the demutualization of the building societies in the 1990s, which had enjoyed great success with its aggressive lending policies, offering some of the best deals on the market. During

2007 it was offering mortgage deals to some clients that were worth six times their annual income. Some of its combined mortgage and personal loan deals were worth 125 per cent of the value of homes. Its ability to offer such attractive terms was dependent on raising a large proportion of its funds from the money markets rather than from depositors. This worked fine when the markets were rising, and confidence was strong. Once the check occurred and the supply of credit dried up, Northern Rock found itself in desperate straits. It could no longer borrow enough to honour the obligations it had undertaken at rates it could afford, so was forced to apply to the Bank of England for emergency financial support. This caused a collapse of confidence in Northern Rock among its depositors, who feared that their money was no longer safe. So began the first bank run in Britain for more than one hundred years. The queues of depositors desperate to get their savings out of the bank which began to form outside Northern Rock branches all over the UK were a harbinger of much worse to come. It shocked the financial establishment and forced the British Government to announce that it would guarantee all the savings in the bank. This was a drastic solution but the alternative was worse, to risk Northern Rock actually becoming bankrupt and the contagion spreading through the UK financial system, with further runs on banks, and huge potential damage to the reputation of UK banking. The actions of the UK authorities were the minimum necessary to stop the financial panic which was engulfing Northern Rock, but at the same time they were trying to intervene as little as possible in the deregulated financial markets, in the hope that the markets would right themselves, and Northern Rock could be kept as an isolated incident.

In the autumn of 2007 the Federal Reserve's strategy for dealing with what was now being called everywhere the 'credit crunch' was an aggressive use of monetary policy, to reduce the price of credit and to inject more funds into the market (see Figure 1.3).

Its main interest rate was cut in September by half a percentage point to 4.75 per cent, and then by quarter percentage rate cuts in October and December 2007 to 4.25 per cent. Even more dramatic cuts were to follow in 2008, starting with two cuts at the end of January 2008, which brought the rate down to 3 per cent. Further reductions followed in March and April bringing the rate down to 2 per cent. Two cuts in October brought it down to 1 per cent, and then in December, a further three quarters percentage rate cut saw the rate hit zero to 0.25 per cent. There was nowhere further to go. This was uncharted territory for the Federal Reserve. The Bank of Japan

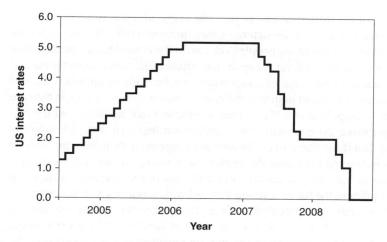

Figure 1.3   US Federal Reserve interest rates, 2005–8

Source: data from Federal Reserve.

had cut rates in the 1990s and eventually reached zero, but by that time the Japanese economy was caught in a downward spiral of deflationary expectations, which even zero interest rates did not break. The steepness of the decline in US rates from 6 per cent in 2007 to 0 per cent by the end of 2008 was remarkable and suggested how worried the authorities were about the consequences if liquidity in the market were to dry up.

Many other central banks followed the example of the Federal Reserve, if much more cautiously, and brought their own rates down. Even the Bank of England, notoriously conservative about interest rates, and throughout most of its history the guardian of a relatively high rate in order to protect the currency, began to aggressively cut rates in 2007, and by the end of 2008 rates had come down to 1.5 per cent; in February 2009 they went to 1 per cent, the lowest ever, and in March 2009 lower still, to 0.5 per cent. There were many critics who regarded this policy as too hasty and too drastic. Given the time lags involved between a rate cut and its impact on spending and saving in the economy, the cuts followed much too quickly to allow an assessment of whether the previous cuts were having any effect. But the authorities brushed this objection aside. They were concerned chiefly with maintaining liquidity in the system, preventing a financial collapse, and making the inevitable recession as shallow and short-lived as possible. In the fog of the markets it was impossible to say who was right. It depended on judgements about the nature of this financial crisis, its causes and its seriousness. Some of the people in charge of the central banks, notably Ben Bernanke at the Federal Reserve, had studied the Great Depression and were adamant the same mistakes would not be made again, when the Fed had actually reduced liquidity and contracted the money supply, in the face of the slump. The result had been a serious price deflation, which had helped make the downturn into a depression that took a decade to overcome. But if the threat of deflation was exaggerated, then reducing interest rates to zero and flooding the markets with money, through the technique known as 'quantitative easing', made the risk of reintroducing inflation at some point in the future a strong possibility. It was a risk that governments were increasingly prepared to face. Ben Bernanke had developed the Bernanke doctrine, based on close study of the 1930s Great Depression. The Bernanke doctrine provided rules for monetary policy to prevent deflation. In a speech in 2002, Bernanke argued that the sources of deflation were not a mystery. Deflation was almost always a side effect of a collapse of aggregate demand. Producers, in response to such a sharp drop in spending, had to cut their prices and then cut them again in order to find buyers. The economic effects of such behaviour would be recession, bankruptcies, rising unemployment and financial stress.

The measures he suggested to combat it included increasing the money supply, ensuring that it resulted in increased liquidity, cutting interest rates – to zero if necessary – depreciating the US dollar and using the power of the Federal Reserve to print money to acquire equity stakes in banks and financial institutions. By 2009 all these policy measures had been adopted, but none of them proved a quick fix.

Cynics noted that resorting to inflation might be the only way governments could possibly alleviate the huge debt burden they had incurred in trying to shore up the financial system. But this itself carried risks. A policy of depreciating both the value of the currency and the value of public debt would undermine the reputation and credibility of governments and financial centres in the advanced economies. If the confidence of key foreign investors and states fell away, the private debt crisis could be replaced by a public debt crisis. Governments and central banks could find it very hard to fund their borrowings, as Iceland found in 2008. Judging where the line lay was far from easy, because no-one had been in this exact place before. Levels of public debt were already high for many countries at the start of the crisis (see Table 1.2).

Table 1.2　Public debt as a percentage of
GDP, 2008 (selected countries)

Japan	170
Italy	104
France	64
Germany	63
United States	61
United Kingdom	47
China	16
Russia	7

Source:　data from CIA, *The World Factbook 2008*.

This dilemma of funding borrowing took some time to emerge. In the early stages of the crash in 2007 and early 2008 the Federal Reserve and the other major central banks did not imagine that they would have to contemplate implementing the Bernanke doctrine in full. Despite the shocks of the failure of Northern Rock and the huge losses being announced by banks like Citigroup and the Swiss Bank UBS (Citigroup alone was to post losses of $40 billion), it was still hoped that modest rate cuts and the announcement by the central banks, orchestrated by the Federal Reserve, in December 2007 of a major loan package to banks, would prove enough. At this stage the Bank of England was still looking for a private sector buyer for Northern Rock, and its interest rate was still at 5.5 per cent (the Fed's rate was 4.25). Governments in several countries were devising packages to help mortgage holders faced with repossession of their homes, but the uncertainty of the outlook was underlined just before Christmas 2007 by Standard and Poor's, one of the world's leading rating agencies, downgrading the credit rating of several insurers of bonds, making it harder for the insurers to repay the loans if the issuer to the bonds defaulted. As so often in this crisis, the problem was not so much the effect on the insurers themselves as the wider effect on the financial markets. It was the realization by the banks that if the insurers were judged no longer able to pay out if the issuers of bonds failed, then another layer of bad debts was potentially uncovered. The longer the crisis went on the more it was like an archaeological dig uncovering layer after layer of bad debts, which no-one had previously suspected, partly because so long as the economy was doing well, there was no reason to regard them as bad debts. Once the market dived, assets that had been considered financially sound suddenly became toxic.

The steady drip of bad news since the summer of 2007 had had a generally lowering effect on stock markets across the world. In January 2008 came the first really steep falls, across all the major markets. The falls were the largest since the aftermath of the 9/11 attacks. It prompted one of the Fed's major rate reductions, which temporarily steadied the markets. But no-one thought the worst was over. It was clear that it was only just beginning. The announcement of major losses, running into billions, by major insurers and banks and other financial institutions, became almost a weekly occurrence, adding to the gloom in the markets, and making everyone more cautious and risk-averse. Everyone, that is, except for governments and central banks, which were now beginning to abandon caution in a desperate bid to restart lending and stop the delicate mechanism of the financial markets, once considered so robust, from stalling.

The casualties kept coming. In February 2008 the British Government announced that Northern Rock would be nationalized. A private buyer had not materialized. The government stressed that Northern Rock would only be in government hands for a temporary period and that, although the government was now directly underwriting all Northern Rock's loans, the exposure of the taxpayer would be limited. But an important precedent had been set. The government had shown it was ready not just to broker a private sector rescue, but to take control itself in certain circumstances. Many questioned why it had taken the government so long, and why this decision could not have been announced the previous September, when Northern Rock first got into difficulties. The answer again turned on judgement. Many government ministers and senior people in the Bank of England had not expected that the crisis was going to worsen in the way it did, and they still could not believe that the engine of the growth model of the last thirty years, the financial services industry, which had been held in such awe for so long, could not be restarted. They kept waiting for it to spring back into life.

The nationalization of Northern Rock in the UK seemed rather minor when, in March, the fifth largest bank on Wall Street, Bear Stearns, was suddenly acquired by JP Morgan Chase. Morgan Chase paid $240 million for a bank which had been valued at $18 billion just one year earlier. If it had waited a few more months it could have had it for even less. This was the speed of the financial collapse which was now beginning to affect some of the best-known names and established businesses on Wall Street and in the City of London. In April, the IMF predicted that losses as a result of the financial crisis could be $1 trillion, and might go higher. It suggested that the losses were now spreading from sub-prime mortgage assets to other sectors, including commercial property, consumer credit and company debt.

No player in the market was immune from this contagion. Even the biggest and most established names began to experience difficulties. A series of rights issues were announced between April and July by major banks to increase the funds available to them; in April the Royal Bank of Scotland announced a £12 billion rights issue, at the same writing £5.9 billion off the value of its investments, the largest ever write-off for a British bank; in May the Swiss Bank UBS announced a $15.5 billion rights issue; and in July Barclays unveiled a £4.5 billion rights issue. The Bank of England and the other central banks, including the ECB, were by now intervening actively in the markets, putting together loan packages, and offering to buy the toxic debt of the banks, later known as TARP (Troubled Assets Relief Programme). But everything was beginning to point down. House prices had begun to slide, along with shares. Banks everywhere were announcing big reductions in their profits and a big increase in their bad debts.

In July the crisis worsened significantly in the US with the collapse first of IndyMac, one of the leading US mortgage lenders, followed the next day by intervention by the authorities to prevent the collapse of Fannie Mae and Freddie Mac, the two mortgage lenders which were the backbone of the US housing market. Several British banks and mortgage lenders looked to be in serious trouble, with attention focused on two former building societies which had been allowed to demutualize and become banks in the 1990s, Bradford and Bingley, and Alliance and Leicester. The authorities appeared to brace themselves for worse news, with warnings being issued by several political leaders and by the OECD about the gloomy economic prospects.

No-one, however, can quite have expected the dramatic events of September 2008. This was an extraordinary month for the global economy. The decisive events again took place in the US. First, on 7 September, Fannie Mae and Freddie Mac had to be bailed out by the Federal authorities, with Hank Paulson, the US Treasury Secretary, declaring that the bad debts which the two mortgage lenders had accumulated posed a systemic risk to the stability of the whole financial system. Then, on 10 September, came the news that Lehman Brothers, one of the world's leading investment banks, had posted a loss of $3.9 billion for the three months to August. It began a desperate search for a buyer, but, on 15 September, was forced to file for bankruptcy. This was the first major bank to go under since the financial crisis began, but the authorities stood back and refused to rescue it. Alan Greenspan called it 'probably a once in a century type of event'. A few more such events were to follow. There was still at this point a strong aversion to a rescue of private sector financial institutions by the government, partly because neo-liberal doctrine held that government had no business in getting involved and would only make things worse, and partly for fear of the signal this would send to the markets. Without the financial discipline of failure and collapse the market could not function as it was intended. This was an ancient problem well known to Adam Smith, which had come to have a new name: moral hazard. If the state was seen to protect against failure, the incentive for market agents to act responsibly would be removed.

The failure of Lehman Brothers seemed to open the floodgates. In quick succession another of the big investment banks, Merrill Lynch, was taken over by Bank of America for $50 billion; the federal authorities stepped in with a $85 billion rescue package for AIG, the biggest insurance company in the US; Wachovia, the fourth largest US bank, was bought by Citigroup, absorbing $42 billion of bad debts. In the UK, HBOS, the country's largest mortgage lender, was taken over by Lloyds TSB, with the encouragement of the government and a promise to waive competition rules, potentially creating a bank which would control one third of the mortgage and saving market; Bradford and Bingley was nationalized; elsewhere in Europe bailouts and partial nationalizations had to be announced for Fortis, Glitnir and Dexia.

Against this background, governments around the world sought to stabilize the situation by agreeing even larger bailouts for their stricken financial systems. The US took the lead in setting out a bipartisan plan to permit the Treasury to spend up to $700 billion buying up the toxic debts on the banks' balance sheets. On 29 September, however, despite frantic last-minute negotiations between the White House and Congressional leaders, the House of Representatives rejected the package. Stock markets promptly collapsed, with Wall Street suffering its largest ever one-day fall; the Dow Jones index was off 770 points or 7 per cent. European governments were forced into competitive declarations of support for the banks, and their depositors, with the Irish Government leading the way in promising it would guarantee all deposits in the country's main banks for two years. The risk of a general collapse in the financial system, with incalculable consequences for the global economy, for a few days appeared very real. George Bush put it bluntly if inelegantly to intransigent Republicans who were refusing to approve the bailout: 'This sucker could go down.' The Senate passed the bailout plan, and then, after the plan had been significantly amended – expanded from twenty to 400 pages – the House of Representatives passed it on 3 October. Other governments around the world followed suit with their own bailouts.

The full extent of what had happened took some time to be recognized. The great boom of the 1990s, powered by the inexorable rise of the deregulated financial markets, had ended with the nationalization of the banks. Governments had been forced to intervene to prevent a complete collapse. The markets had been unable to save or regulate themselves. The Iceland Government took control of Landsbanki, the country's second largest bank, Germany injected €50 billion into its banks, the UK announced its own rescue package of £50 billion on 8 October to recapitalize the banks, and a further £200 billion in short-term loans. There were similar rescue packages announced by Sweden, the Netherlands and France. Interest rates were slashed again in Washington, London and also in India. China too became concerned about the backwash of the financial crash on its economy and announced a major fiscal stimulus.

Despite these unprecedented moves, or perhaps because of them, the markets continued to slide. Expectations of a deep depression were now almost universal and the action by the central banks in cutting interest rates to such low levels, despite the relatively high rates of inflation, convinced the markets that the authorities themselves were now anticipating a sharp downturn in economic activity and were desperately trying to mitigate its effects and prevent it from turning into a major deflation, with the serious consequences for all economies that would bring. Figures on employment, prices and consumer confidence were enough to trigger further falls in stock market prices. On 15 October, the Dow Jones index fell 733 points, 7.8 per cent, even outdoing the fall in September.

International diplomacy was also now in full swing. A meeting of G7 finance ministers in Washington on 11 October issued a five-point plan of action to unfreeze the credit markets, and there was agreement that every country should do all in its power to reduce interest rates, recapitalize the banks and provide a fiscal stimulus to keep economic activity from plunging. This was followed up by the US Government announcing a $250 billion package to purchase stakes in US banks, and the UK Government agreeing deals with three of the largest British banks – Royal Bank of Scotland, Lloyds TSB, and HBOS – to receive £37 billion.

Action to sustain liquidity and shore up the banks was increasingly accompanied by fiscal boosts to maintain the level of demand and prevent a descent into slump. China's announcement, on 9 November, that it would provide $568 billion over two years was particularly significant. It reflected widespread awareness of the perils that were now facing the global economy. Even the European Central Bank, which had been noticeably more cautious in responding to the crisis, was steadily reducing its interest rates, down to 3.25 per cent on 6 November. The eurozone economy had already entered recession, and everyone recognized it was only a matter of time before the US and UK economies did too.

Right up to the end of 2008 more news of bank rescues and fiscal packages kept coming. The IMF announced a major rescue for Iceland following the earlier collapse of the Icelandic banking system, and a few weeks later for Pakistan. Citigroup was rescued by the US Government after its share price collapsed, and the UK Government, in its pre-Budget Report in November, predicted that the effects of the bank bailouts and fiscal stimulus would require record borrowing. VAT was reduced by 2.5 per cent, a £12 billion injection. The government promised that the record borrowing would be temporary, designed to ward off the recession, and that as soon as the worst was over, taxes would have to rise and public spending be cut, in order to rebuild the public finances. These assurances were necessary because, with flexible exchange rates, those countries like Iceland and the UK which had very large financial sectors in relation to the rest of their economy were highly vulnerable to speculators losing confidence in the currency. Both the dollar and the eurozone were relatively insulated, the dollar because of its status as the reserve currency of the global economy. But the pound was highly exposed and, at the end of 2008, began to fall sharply against the euro and the yen, and to a lesser extent against the dollar.

Even countries that had seemed unaffected began to be caught up in the general problems. Australia had looked as though it would escape the worst of the crash and the downturn. Mineral exports had remained buoyant, and Australian banks had not been heavily involved in the international credit boom, and were not exposed to huge losses when the sub-prime market turned down. Australia had, however, seen very large rises in house prices, and it was dependent on the inflow of funds from foreign banks. When the international financial system crashed, overseas banks began to repatriate funds and, at the end of 2008, Australia suddenly faced a slowing economy, a stock market crash and anxieties about how it was going to fund the shortfall in its banking system. Australia was one of the first victims of the new phenomenon of financial protectionism, the unwillingness of banks to lend outside their own economies. The Australian Government responded with a package of measures, including an AS\$4 billion business investment partnership, to plug the hole in the banks' accounts created by the withdrawal of foreign bank funds. In this way it was hoped Australia could insulate itself from the worst of the recession and the banking crisis in the rest of the world.

2008 ended with more dramatic decisions in the United States. The Federal Reserve brought interest rates down to zero and the US Government moved to bail out its loss-making car industry, Ford, GM and Chrysler, and save them from bankruptcy. There was clearly much more to come, but at the end of 2008 it did at least appear that swift and decisive action by governments had staved off the complete collapse of the financial system, but with unknown consequences for the rest of the economy. Governments had been forced to address problems which were unprecedented, and for which there were, therefore, no exact or reliable guides from the past. Steve Forbes, proprietor of *Forbes Magazine*, flamboyant financier, prominent neo-conservative and supply-sider, economic policy adviser to John McCain, having run for the Presidency twice himself, declared on 28 October that 'the worst was over', and that the US economy would quickly bounce back. But no-one could be sure. In the Great Crash, Herbert Hoover had been much mocked for announcing that 'prosperity was just round the corner'. It was, but it turned out to be a very long corner.

2
Crises of Capitalism

By the beginning of 2009 it was clear that the global economy was facing a major recession. Several of the leading economies were already in recession and the question was how deep the recession would be and how long it would persist, and whether the world could avoid something still worse, the kind of depression which the United States experienced in the 1930s or Japan in the 1990s. The IMF report published in January 2009 predicted that the recession for the advanced economies was likely to be the worst since the 1930s, with a drop in output of 2 per cent (see Table 2.1).

Table 2.1 Percentage changes in GDP, 2007 and 2008, and projected changes, 2009 and 2010

	2007	2008	2009	2010
World output	**5.2**	**4.3**	**0.5**	**3.0**
All advanced economies	**2.7**	**1.0**	**-2.0**	**1.1**
United States	2.0	1.1	-1.6	1.6
Eurozone	2.6	1.0	-2.0	0.2
Germany	2.5	1.3	-2.5	0.1
United Kingdom	3.0	0.7	-2.8	0.2
Japan	2.4	-0.3	-2.8	0.2
All emerging and developing economies	**8.3**	**6.3**	**3.3**	**5.0**
Africa	6.2	5.2	3.4	4.9
Russia	8.1	6.2	-0.7	1.3
China	13.0	9.0	6.7	8.0
India	9.3	7.3	5.1	6.5
Brazil	5.7	5.8	1.8	3.5

Source: data from IMF *World Economic Report*, January 2009.

If realized this would be the first time there had been an overall aggregate economic contraction for those economies during the post-war period, with the cumulative output loss being equivalent to the 1974–5 and 1980–2 recessions. The rising economic powers, especially India, China and Brazil, were expected to continue to grow through the recession but at sharply reduced rates, pulling the forecast for the growth of total world output down to 0.5 per cent. The countries expected to be hardest hit in 2009 were Britain, expected to decline by 2.8 per cent, Japan, by 2.6 per cent, and Germany, by 2.5 per cent. The United States was expected to decline by 1.6 per cent and the euro area as a whole by 2.0 per cent. Recovery was predicted for 2010, with world economic growth increasing by 3 per cent, but many of the advanced economies were predicted to have weak growth, and it was expected that some of them, including Italy and Spain, would still be contracting. This was not expected to be the last word. All these predictions had been marked down sharply since the IMF's previous world economic outlook six months before, and further downward revisions during 2009 were highly likely. Individual countries began publishing very gloomy forecasts of their prospects, amid fears that in some cases the drop in output could be worse than that experienced in 1929–32.

Recessions are not the normal condition of capitalism or the expected condition of democracy, both of which thrive on optimism and progress, the sense that things can get better, and will get better. The great booms of capitalism have thrived on exuberance, and the readiness to take risks and to embrace change. The longer a boom lasts the more complacent and careless many people become, from those in charge of governments and banks down to the humblest investor. The calculations of risk change. By degrees everyone comes to believe that the boom will last for ever, and that, finally, the secret of everlasting growth has been discovered. The recession comes as a shock. It punctures expectations about what is normal and forces everyone to reassess not just their investments and their prospects, but also their assumptions about how to operate in markets. But some recessions are different. They trigger a more profound political and economic crisis, a crisis which concerns both the legitimacy of the political and economic order, the presumed social contract that underlies it and the distribution of power, both within national political systems and between them in the international state system.

The financial crash of 2007/8 and the recession which it engendered is the first major crisis of capitalism in this sense since the 1970s, but where on the scale of past capitalist crises it will eventually be judged to lie cannot yet be known. It is still unfolding and its consequences will take time to be understood. The pessimists, like the New York economist Nouriel Roubini, have so far proved more right about the course of this present crisis than the optimists, but that does not mean that the gloomiest scenarios will turn out to be true. What everyone now acknowledges, after the tense days in September 2008, is that this crisis has the potential to match in importance the two great capitalist crises of the twentieth century – the Great Depression of the 1930s and the 1970s stagflation. How serious it will turn out to be, however, will depend on the responses of a multitude of people across the global economy: decision-makers in governments, banks and companies; political parties, social movements and pressure groups; and ordinary consumers and citizens. A crisis is not a natural event, but a social event, and therefore is always socially constructed and highly political. The narratives that are used to designate an event or a period as a crisis imply certain courses of action, and privilege some responses over others. This crisis is no different.

Crisis has not always been thought of in this way. For much of the history of capitalism, crises were considered to be more natural events than political events, brought about by economic laws rather than by political actions. This perspective was itself an important way in which crises were explained and in determining the response to them. At a certain point in the development of the modern capitalist economy, however, this perception changed and the role of the states in managing and if possible preventing capitalist crises came to the fore. This chapter considers some of the events and the thinkers who were important in that shift.

The Meaning of Crisis

Crisis is a much overused term, but still an indispensable one. It is used in many different senses and has acquired a number of different meanings. One of the oldest uses of the term is medical; the crisis is a moment of danger but also of opportunity, the point in the progress of a disease when a change takes place which is decisive for recovery or death. Here crisis is understood as a distinct moment in a process which has a much longer time frame. This process is the disease itself, and the crisis is the turning point in that disease, the moment when the body either starts to shake off the disease or succumbs to it.

This notion of crisis as the point of resolution is also present in drama and music. Plays are often structured so that they build to a climax, which is then resolved in a way that makes sense of everything that has happened up to that point. The notion of crisis as a turning point is evident again here, the moment when a decisive change for better or worse is imminent. The conception of crisis in drama also suggests a very important feature of social and political crises which goes beyond the medical analogy. Crises are constructed by particular narratives and interpretations of events, which legitimate particular ways of resolving them. In this view an economic crisis is not just something that impinges on us with the force of a natural event. It is something we construct for ourselves.

Another very important aspect of crisis is that it always involves an element of suspense. In a crisis people are waiting to see what will happen. Both the medical and the dramatic meanings of crisis imply that crises are contingent, that their outcome is not fore-ordained, and that there is more than one way in which they might be resolved. To call a situation critical is to suggest that it involves imminent danger and high risk. Decisions have to be taken under pressure with very incomplete knowledge and can lead to very different results. The pilot forced to make an emergency landing after engine failure makes decisions which may determine whether the passengers live or die. It is the element of choice and contingency as much as that of danger which makes us define a situation as critical.

The term can also be used in a much more prosaic way simply to mean an emergency; any sudden or unexpected event which poses a severe challenge to a family, to an organization, or to a state. Daily life is littered with crises in this sense, but it empties the term of most of its distinctiveness. A humanitarian catastrophe like the tsunami in 2004 certainly created an emergency but hardly a crisis in the deeper sense being employed here. It required rapid mobilization of relief efforts around the world and in the countries most concerned. There were criticisms that the emergency services and the aid relief might have been better prepared and might have responded more quickly. But these were related to the event as a natural emergency rather than as a political emergency and therefore a crisis.

A crisis as a political emergency, a critical event demanding an immediate response, is perhaps the most widespread use of the term. The events in the financial markets following the collapse of Lehman Brothers in September 2008 created a political emergency and some instant action by governments around the world. This crisis was quickly over. There is another use of the term, however, mainly by historians and social scientists, to mean a much more deep-seated impasse in an organization, a society, or a state. Here crisis is used to refer not just to the turning point of a particular historical process but also to a set of historical events, which may take place over quite long time-spans. To talk of the crisis of the Roman Empire, for example, directs attention not just to a single event which proved decisive for the destruction of that empire, but to a long, protracted process of conflict, recovery and decline. The term 'crisis' assumes a structural character – it refers here to an impasse, or deadlock, in a society or institution, which can persist for a very long time before it is decisively resolved. A crisis can mean a very involved and complicated stand-off, with moments of drama and activity oscillating with longer periods of immobility. We identify such crises retrospectively, when we know the final outcome. The Roman Empire did collapse. It was unable to overcome its crisis. All we are left with are its ruins, its legacies and its memory. But at the time it is often hard for contemporaries to know how serious the crisis is through which they are living and different judgements will be made and different courses of action advocated. What makes it a crisis is that even in periods of relative calm the underlying causes and conflicts which give rise to dramatic episodes and decisive confrontations have not gone away. They can suddenly erupt with terrifying force. It is these eruptions which retrospectively allow the whole phenomenon to be labelled a crisis, and allow the different symptoms to be identified and understood in the context of the whole.

This historians' understanding of crisis is a world away from many journalists' or politicians' understanding of crisis. For the latter, crises are often daily, and mainly ephemeral, measured by the number of days a story stays in the headlines. What makes an event a crisis is that it creates a sudden operational emergency, which has to be handled and defused immediately. Politicians are judged by how well they perform in such fire-fighting, how quickly they respond, how effectively they deal with whatever problem has suddenly arisen, and whether they stay in control of the news agenda or cede it to their opponents. Journalists spend much of their time looking for new crises, while the politicians spend a great deal of theirs attempting to smother them, or preventing them from ever arising in the first place. But, given the plentiful supply of such crises, many of them manufactured by the news industry itself, their efforts are only partially successful. Out of the fog of events gradually there emerge the narratives that come to construct the bigger pictures and the frameworks which everybody comes to rely on to understand what is going on.

The global financial crash of 2007/8 has been constructed as a crisis in a number of different ways from the beginning. The term 'global financial crash' itself describes a process which has many individual incidents; at the same time there has been much comment on whether this or that event is the decisive moment, whether symbolically – the failure to rescue Lehman Brothers in September 2008; or actually – the turning point that marks the low point in the cycle and the beginnings of recovery. It was common in past capitalist crises for many different turning points to be identified, but they were not the real one.They generated short-lived bursts of optimism and recovery, before the market slumped again and resumed its inexorable downward path.

Political and economic events are extremely complex phenomena, and our knowledge is highly provisional and very incomplete. The methodologies of natural science have often been applied to the study of society, but the knowledge gained as a result is severely limited. It will always fall short of the precise and reliable knowledge that has been gained about the natural world, both in completeness or in utility, because the social world is unlike the natural world in the key sense that in the social world the way human beings perceive events forms part of the reality that social scientists are trying to explain. The making of predictions can alter behaviour in ways that falsifies the predictions, and generalizing from the past can mistake the way the context has altered which can make the knowledge that has been gained no longer applicable. Many social scientists have believed that there is an objective social reality quite independent of human perceptions of it. Some strands of contemporary economics, such as that involved in the failure of the hedge fund, Long Term Capital Management in 1997, have moved in that direction, forgetting Keynes' warnings about the hazards of making predictions about the way in which markets move. He always insisted on the extreme precariousness of the estimates we could make about prospective yields of investments or the future performance of the economy, because of the necessary incompleteness of our knowledge.

The complexity of social phenomena means that anyone seeking to understand what is going on in a global financial crisis finds that, while the range of disagreement can be reduced, there will always be a number of arguments, models and perspectives which offer different accounts, which all have greater or lesser plausibility and are more or less consistent with the evidence. Some arguments do get weeded out, or wither away over time, but it is remarkable how many arguments in political economy survive, not just in the academy, but also in popular discourses and the discourses of politics. The ideas of Adam Smith, of Karl Marx, of Joseph Schumpeter, of Friedrich Hayek, of John Maynard Keynes and many more are still with us, and some of them are explored below. They have generated a rich literature on capitalist crisis, its causes, its origins, its consequences and its remedies. Many of the ideas that are expressed are still current and are still being used to understand the nature of the political and economic reality we inhabit.

The lack of definitive knowledge and the presence of many competing discourses adds to the fog of events. Trying to decide when a crisis is really a crisis, and when a turning point might or might not have been reached, and what the causes and consequences of a crisis may be, is far from simple. This book does not attempt to offer a definitive account of the crisis, its causes and consequences. It can only offer a view of events from a particular perspective, which has limitations, as do all perspectives, arising from a particular place and a particular time.

The argument of this book is that the credit crunch of 2007, the financial crash of 2008 and the recession of 2009 are all aspects of a much wider crisis, a crisis which has come about because of flaws in the growth model which helped propel the global economy out of its last major downturn, and because of broader shifts in power that are taking place in the global political economy. It faces us with a new and daunting set of political challenges. This crisis can be viewed from a number of perspectives: as a crisis of the banking system, as a crisis of regulation, as a crisis of the continued hegemony of the United States over the global economy and as a political crisis of the legitimacy of the global order. Taken together these add up to something once very familiar, but now less so, the idea of a crisis of capitalism. This book explores how this spectre from the past has come back to haunt today's global economy. I say 'spectre from the past' because, until the global financial crisis of 2008, it was widely held that capitalist crisis would not return. These claims first began to be made in the 1960s with the great post-war boom still in full flow, and the privations of the Great Depression in the 1930s and of the World War a receding memory. They were checked by the first post-war global recession in 1974–5 and its distinctive combination of high unemployment and high inflation. This was recognizably a capitalist crisis, but it was heavily managed and, although the stagnation lasted several years, it was relatively short-lived, in comparison to the 1930s. Political responses to the crisis gradually paved the way for a new regime, a new growth model and a new world order, which eventually resolved the crisis, and it was not long before the claims, that capitalism no longer had to worry about the spectre of crisis coming back, began again. There continued to be many small crises, but none of them seemed to pose dangers for the system as a whole, and were successfully confined to national or to regional level.

Early Forms of Capitalist Crisis

This confidence in the ability of governments and central banks to manage the global economy and preserve reasonable stability and progress within it has not always existed, and certainly did not exist in some earlier periods of capitalist development. Indeed, the idea that the process of capital accumulation could be managed at all was once an alien one. The capitalist economy and its violent cycles of boom and slump were regarded with wonderment as something spectacular and novel. The novelty lay in the fact that, unlike the crises of the agricultural economy which were natural disasters, the slumps of capitalism were man-made. The Lisbon earthquake of 1755, which killed up to 40,000 people and made such a deep impression on Voltaire, so much so that it becomes a central event in *Candide*, was the kind of natural disaster with which everyone was familiar. But thirty years before, in 1720, there had been the South Sea Bubble, an extraordinary man-made event in which many thousands of investors were ruined, hoping to get rich by investing in a project which proved to be worthless. The power which free markets could unleash, the dreams of unlimited wealth, the scramble to take part, the suddenness of the collapse and the utter ruin of so many of the participants, made a lasting impression. It was not just the natural elements human beings had to fear. They had to fear the destructive powers of social institutions they themselves had created.

These early financial crises of capitalism tended to be sporadic and local. They were the subject of much moralizing and anxiety, but at the same time they were widely accepted as part of the new urban commercial society, and excused as the product of exuberance. Restrictions on joint stock companies were tightened, which delayed their progress in Britain for more than a century, but there was no serious attempt to roll back the banking and financial revolution. As the new industries developed and the market network broadened and deepened, so the extraordinary ability of capitalism to increase wealth grew, not just in huge speculative frenzies like the South Sea Bubble, but incrementally, and steadily, and seemingly indefinitely. In the pre-industrial era economic output increased slowly, if at all, in many societies, and there were many setbacks. In the last two hundred years, growth both of output and population has accelerated and become a normal expectation in more and more parts of the world. In the future it is likely to accelerate even more.

It took a long time for this change to register properly, and it was not until well into the nineteenth century that the full implications and consequences of this economic revolution began to be understood. By then it was also clear that periodic speculative crises were not singular, disconnected events, but arose spontaneously from the production cycle of capitalism itself. The rhythm of capitalist production meant a long, sustained upswing, which lasted several years, increasing production and profits and employment, but then ending in a sharp downturn marked by collapsing prices and share values, bankruptcies, employment – factories and workers idle and trade depressed. After a short period of depression, a new upswing would begin. What made these business cycles tolerable was that the loss of value in the slump never wiped out all the value that had previously been created. The economy would always resume its growth from a higher level than at the start of the previous cycle, so that the general impression and the reality was one of continuing progress, and expanding wealth, even if this was extremely unequally distributed among those with property and those without.

The rhythm of the business cycle and the violence of its fluctuations came to be seen both by the friends and the enemies of capitalism as intrinsic to it. Commercial crises were man-made but they were often treated as though they were natural phenomena, like bad harvests. No-one thought much could be done about them, or should be done about them. Socialists vowed to abolish them by abolishing capitalism and organizing the production of wealth along collective rather than individual lines. They did not think capitalism could be reformed in ways that might make the incidence of these crises less or mitigate the effects on those thrown out of work and into destitution. Crises and capitalism became inextricably linked in the minds of socialists. This was a form of political economy which created huge wealth but at huge cost. Capitalism could only progress and renew itself through this regular purging of its excesses in a slump of the values that had been created. The brunt of these adjustments was borne by the working class in the shape of poverty, destitution, unemployment, malnutrition, poor health and limited education. For socialists this provided a compelling moral and pragmatic case for getting rid of capitalism altogether. Their account of capitalist crisis highlighted the human cost of these violent oscillations in economic activity and argued that the institutions which made such oscillations possible should be abolished.

Those better disposed towards capitalism came to different conclusions, but they too tended to think of capitalism as part of a natural social order which was not dependent on government for its success, and which possessed its own internal laws which governments should respect but could not alter. Many of the classical liberal economists conceived the nineteenth-century capitalist economy as Newton conceived the universe – a marvellously intricate piece of machinery, which, once set in motion, ran itself. It might be observed and analysed, but it did not need any steering or control, and any attempt to provide such steering might well upset the delicate mechanism. It worked according to iron and inescapable laws.

In the nineteenth century this attitude became entrenched in political economy, partly through the development of more abstract theoretical models of the economy by David Ricardo and others. It exerted a powerful pull over all political economists, including Marx. The political aspect of political economy was not given much prominence, although there was a strand of thought, represented by John Stuart Mill, which did point in a different direction. As a leading representative of the English school of political economy, which drew on the tradition of the classical political economy represented by David Ricardo, as well as on the utilitarianism of Jeremy Bentham, Mill shared the belief that there were natural economic laws which could be discovered by rational enquiry, but unlike some of his contemporaries he believed a distinction could be drawn between the natural laws governing production and the social laws governing distribution. The first might be unalterable, but the second were not. They could be improved and reformed to suit human purposes. Mill developed a strand of political economy inherited from the Scottish political economy school of Adam Smith and David Hume, which had an interest in practical issues concerning the role government should play in the economy. This pragmatic, flexible, discretionary approach to economic problems increasingly came to see the capitalist business cycle as something that was a suitable target for government intervention to moderate if it could. It tended to see the main task of political economy to be devising the most effective policies for the preservation of the market system. Mill kept alive and helped develop a way of thinking about economic problems which was eventually to lead to the political economy of the new Liberals in the first half of the twentieth century, prominent among whom was John Maynard Keynes.

A very different tradition of political economy emerged in Vienna, the Austrian school, founded by Carl Menger in the second half of the nineteenth century and continued by Eugen von Böhm Bawerk, Ludwig von Mises and Friedrich Hayek in the twentieth. Austrians defended the market as a spontaneous order which had arisen independently of government, and with which government should not interfere. The capitalist market economy was a precious legacy which underpinned the foundations of modern civilization. Hayek argued that without it the population of the world could never have grown as it had in the last two hundred years, and if it were suddenly to disappear this population could no longer be supported.

For the Austrians the business cycle had a necessary and important function within capitalism. The crisis phase of the cycle was crucial if capitalism was to renew itself, and purge itself of the false values and the misallocated productive resources which had grown up during the boom phase. The crisis was a moment of truth, when suddenly the plans and the claims and the expectations which had been formed during the upswing were put to the test. Many of them would be found wanting, and those responsible for them would have to face the consequences. This process was not just necessary to keep capitalism efficient, it was also necessary to keep capitalism moral. Only if market agents bore full responsibility for their actions would the values of prudence, reliability, sound judgement and trust, on which capitalism relied, be upheld. The crisis purged capitalism in a double sense – both practically and morally. To many of its defenders the two were equally important. It was what gave capitalism its practical dynamism and its moral legitimacy. Like the socialist account of crisis this liberal account was a particular way of constructing it and understanding it, and carried implications for the politics of the crisis, in deciding what was an appropriate and what was an inappropriate response.

Marx and the Capitalist Business Cycle

Classical Marxists were closer to Austrians in the way they thought about political economy than they were to Mill. Marx himself was strongly influenced by Ricardo, and agreed with the classical liberal claim that crises were an unavoidable product of the rhythm of the business cycle. Marx studied capitalist crises in the nineteenth century, particularly in Britain, and from his vantage point in the Reading Room of the British Museum, these cataclysmic events made a deep impression on him. He fashioned one of the first and most influential theories of the capitalist business cycle, stressing how capitalists were driven through the competitive character of the accumulation process always to create an overproduction both of consumer goods and of productive capacity. At a certain point in the cycle this overproduction would cause a collapse of profits and trigger a slump. There have always been debates among Marxists about whether the fundamental cause of capitalist crisis was overproduction or underconsumption. Was the problem that profits were too low to continue expanding production, or was it that there was insufficient demand to buy the products? Marx himself always believed that the fundamental problem was maintaining a high enough rate of profit at the top of the boom to make it worth continuing to invest. Once investment and the growth of production faltered, financial values would be affected, and markets would start plunging. The complex web of finance built up to smooth the transfer of funds between different sectors and levels was immensely efficient both in supporting the boom and in facilitating the slump. The financial sector allowed values to be created which diverged from production values. What counted was whether market agents believed in these values and were prepared to enter the market and trade on the basis of them. The values in the market therefore depended in part on the perceptions of these agents, and when those perceptions changed this helped cause the great oscillations in markets that were observed, and the rise and fall of expectations.

Marx analysed all aspects of the capitalist business cycle. He was particularly fascinated by the detachment of finance from production, and the consequences of an independent world of fictitious paper values which derived from the values created in production, but increasingly floated free from it, and became the purest form of capital. He analysed with great acuity the build-up to each great commercial crisis, and the behaviour of the various market agents, all striving to maximize their returns, and in doing so making the overreaching and the lurch into overproduction and then slump inevitable. Marx also thought it inevitable that the brunt of each crisis would be borne by the working class, in an era before unemployment insurance and very limited forms of welfare. One of the problems of the boom for capital, according to Marx, was precisely that during it labour became scarce as more and more workers were absorbed into employment, and this led to wages being bid up, helping to squeeze profits and to make further investment less profitable. One of the key functions of the crisis for Marx was to reconstitute what he called the reserve army of labour, by making thousands of workers unemployed again and driving down wages in the general price deflation that always ensued. With wages low again and a plentiful supply of workers available again, employers could begin to invest and expand production in the knowledge that their labour costs at least would remain low and under control in the early years of the new upswing.

Marx was an incurable optimist when it came to politics, and managed to convince himself, in defiance of his economic analysis, that capitalist crises were becoming so violent that the next one might be capitalism's last. The predictions of the *Communist Manifesto* would come true. The spectre that had been haunting Europe, the spectre of communism, would take shape in the working class. Capitalism would confront its gravediggers. The propertyless would rise against the propertied and refuse to accept the injustices and cruelties to which the capitalist production process and the capitalist business cycle subjected them. Marx's political position in the end was the opposite of the Austrians, although he would have agreed with their economic analysis on many points. For Marx, capitalism stood condemned morally, because of the way it treated the great bulk of the population, as well as practically, because at a certain point capitalism could no longer renew itself and continue to develop the economy.

As a radical revolutionary Marx thought the sooner capitalism was gone the better. He fretted in correspondence to Engels during the great commercial crisis of 1857 in Britain that the revolution might take place before he had had a chance to finish writing *Capital*, which was to lay bare the secret of its working, and provide the principles to guide the working-class movement in opposing and replacing it. But he need not have worried. His own analysis pointed in a different direction. It had emerged in the course of his extraordinary detailed studies in the 1850s and was to be published first in volume one of *Capital,* later in the two volumes published by Engels after Marx's death, later still in the *Theories of Surplus Value,* edited by Kautsky, and, finally, in the unfinished *Grundrisse*, which provided a sketch of Marx's whole plan and grand design which he never lived to execute.

Despite himself, Marx moved away from the revolutionary opportunism of the *Communist Manifesto*, with its radical call to all working men to unite and overthrow their oppressors. In his later writings he developed a deep appreciation of the scope and scale of capitalism as a system of production, and of its huge potential, even if he never fully reconciled this with his own political hopes. His analysis suggested that capitalism could go on renewing itself through successive cycles of boom, crisis and slump until it had exhausted all room for further investment and opportunities for profitable accumulation, and that the pragmatic as opposed to the moral case for replacing capitalism would not arise until alternatives to capitalism were already present within it, and capitalism was visibly becoming less and less able to function successfully. But if Marx was correct, that would not occur until a fully globalized economy had been created, with all nations and all territories drawn fully into capitalist production, in which production methods had advanced to the point where most production processes were fully automated, and most of the population had become surplus to the requirements of the production process. One hundred and fifty years later Marx can be credited with huge prescience in certain respects about the course modern capitalism would take, but even now the job is only half done. In terms of Marx's own analysis, capitalism still has a long way to go before the possibilities of profitable capital accumulation are exhausted. The entry of China and India as full players in the global capitalist economy is still very recent, and many parts of the Global South remain marginal to the global economy.

From a classical Marxist perspective, as from a classical Austrian perspective, we might therefore expect the cycle of boom, crash and slump to persist almost indefinitely as the institutional means by which this mode of production both generates wealth and renews its ability to do so. It is the dynamism of capitalism, its creativity as well as its destructiveness, which sets it apart from every other economic system known in human history, and which has underpinned modernity. Marx thought that eventually capitalism would self-destruct; the Austrians believed this would only happen if there was deliberate political interference in the way it operated. Both believed that capitalism resembled a force of nature. Once established, capitalism worked in a very particular manner, and it worked as a whole. As Marx put in the preface to *Capital*, it is a question of 'the natural laws of capitalist production ... of these tendencies winning their way through and working themselves out with iron necessity' (Marx, 1976, p. 91). The Austrians believed in natural laws too, if rather different ones.

Crises in the Twentieth Century

Joseph Schumpeter had a major influence on twentieth-century political economy through his attempts to understand the new stage which capitalism had reached. He spent his early life in Vienna and Bonn, and the latter part of his life in Harvard. Although schooled in the Austrian tradition, he never fully belonged to it, but he was always scornful of the English school of political economy and of Keynes. Although he had strongly disagreed politically with Marx he admired his achievement, and particularly his theory of the capitalist business cycle. He, more than anyone, summed up this particular Austrian/Marxist view of capitalist crisis. Drawing on both Marx and Menger, he described the strength of capitalism, the process of creative destruction it unleashed, its restless dynamism, its ability to give incentives to entrepreneurs to search out new profitable opportunities, and develop new businesses, to exploit new technologies and constantly innovate in the search for profit. Such a system, he acknowledged, was extraordinarily wasteful and destructive, occasionally brutal, morally questionable and culturally illegitimate, but it had produced, he argued, the most glittering civilization in human history, nineteenth-century Europe. The bad sides of capitalism, among which he included the human and social costs of the periodic slumps, were, however, not optional. It was the price which had to be paid for the benefits.

Schumpeter lived through the first half of the twentieth century, during two world wars and the Great Depression, the rise of collectivism and the gradual spread of democracy. He was a conservative and a pessimist and, unlike Friedrich Hayek and Marx, he thought that capitalism could not survive in its present form. 'Will capitalism survive? No I do not think it can', he famously declared in *Capitalism, Socialism and Democracy* (Schumpeter, 1976, p. 61). It was not that he wanted to see it disappear. On the contrary. But he thought that the conditions for successful capitalism, and in particular for ensuring that the process of creative destruction was allowed to flourish unchecked, were dwindling. He was very critical of the policies of Roosevelt's New Deal. He foresaw a future in which capitalist economies would be socialized, not in the way Marx had predicted, but through the growth of elitist democracy on the one hand and bureaucratic state collectivism on the other. The two forces would come together to protect living standards and employment and maintain industrial efficiency, but at the expense of dynamism, creativity and individualism. Economies would henceforward be dominated by large public corporations, many of them directly controlled by the state, and run by the new class of salaried managers, politicians and bureaucrats. He might have added regulators and pension fund managers. In this way, capitalist crises, and capitalism itself, would become a thing of the past. Schumpeter saw no alternative to economies in the future being bureaucratized and collectivist. They would not be run by the people but by elites, including the political elite, which would be selected through the institutional arrangement of rival teams of leaders competing against one another periodically to have the right to take control of the executive. This, he declared, was what democracy meant in the modern world, and the only kind of democracy that was possible. In those states where it had acquired any kind of foothold, this was what democracy amounted to.

Schumpeter believed that capitalism was slowly being transformed into a different kind of economic system, and that the workings of this new system would remove the need for capitalist crisis. He personally deplored this development, and was a strong critic of Keynes for helping to legitimize it. During the Great Depression Schumpeter favoured the classical liberal position of letting things take their course, letting the economy be purged of its toxic debts and misallocated resources, and allowing the basis for a new capitalist upsurge to be created. Keynes advocated policies which would suppress the crisis and damp down the fluctuations of the cycle. This would please the new democratic electorates but it would remove the distinctive mechanism which had allowed capitalism to achieve such spectacular economic development in the past. Schumpeter did not doubt that such a policy was possible, but he still regretted it.

Schumpeter was wrong about the inability of capitalism to renew itself, and he failed to foresee the new upsurges created by entrepreneurial dynamism and innovation that would be possible even under a much more bureaucratic capitalism. But he was not wrong in thinking that the state would be much more interventionist, or that the state sector would be permanently enlarged or that democracy would have lasting effects on the political management of capitalism, and would seek to manage capitalist crises and if possible suppress them. He recognized very clearly the different institutional setting of capitalism in the twentieth century, and how it had evolved into a different kind of society. The changing attitude to crisis and the business cycle was one of its manifestations.

Karl Polanyi was a close contemporary of Schumpeter, and came to some of the same conclusions, but from a political perspective that welcomed the growth of state intervention as a necessary correction to the shortcomings of free market capitalism in the nineteenth century. In *The Great Transformation*, first published in 1944, he argued that the liberal political economy of the nineteenth century had not been a spontaneous natural order at all, but had been a deliberate creation of policy. It had broken traditional society and instituted new disciplines and new institutions, which had produced great achievements and progress but also great dislocation and suffering. Capitalist crises might appear as natural events, but they were actually deliberate acts of human will. Setting economic activity free had led to huge inequalities and suffering in society, and in time had produced strong political reaction. Social movements on both right and left arose to demand greater security, the imposition of minimum levels of income and welfare, and the control of the capitalist business cycle. Gradually the new collectivism won through, imposing new regulations on the enormously powerful capitalist economy, setting out new social priorities, and taming the market. Controlling the destructive capitalist economic cycle was one of the chief aims of this new politics, ending the periodic slumps and mass unemployment, with all the attendant social distress it caused. Polanyi believed that the future lay with either a highly regulated and ordered form of capitalism, or with various forms of socialism. What would not be permitted again would be the kind of capitalist crisis which had erupted in 1929, and caused such devastation.

Marx's original account of capitalist crisis had been based on detailed observation of the decennial business cycle of the capitalism of his time, but behind this account lay a broader vision of a political crisis of capitalism which one of these commercial crises might trigger, but would be altogether a much larger political, ideological and economic event. One important strand of his work suggested that capitalism would always tend to create such systemic crises as it developed, because of its highly unstable character and the conflicts endemic within it, but the way such crises were resolved would depend on politics, and the will and capacity of the different classes.

This way of understanding crises bequeathed a very different legacy to his followers. Polanyi developed the insights of this more political Marx, while Schumpeter preferred the Ricardian Marx. For those who thought like Polanyi it was clear that the political construction of crises was in itself a powerful political instrument. Were these events which had such devastating implications for so many lives an unavoidable part of a spontaneous order, a price worth paying for the wealth, freedoms and security of modern society, or were they outrages about which something can and should be done? Very different answers were given in the first half of the twentieth century and continue to be given. What all these accounts shared was the conviction that these economic events mattered politically. As societies grew more interdependent and the effects of economic downturns were experienced very widely, so the political construction of these events as crises came to matter more, and calls grew for a political response to them. Government could not absolve itself of responsibility. Seeing crises as political events and not just economic events brought into sharp focus the question of whether crises might be avoided by government action, and whose interests were served in the different proposals made for handling them.

Political theories of crisis also brought out the contingent nature of crisis. Once the underlying economic and political situation was designated a crisis, it could be shaped in various ways. Many different interests, circumstances and ideas could be brought into play, and no set of actors was guaranteed the outcome they favoured. The realization of how complex the economic relationships of the modern world had become, coupled with the extreme fragility of the political relationships which underpinned them both at national but particularly and increasingly at international level, brought a certain wonder that the capitalist economy worked as well as it did, and broke down relatively infrequently. But whenever it did break down recovery now seemed increasingly difficult and to require greater and greater state involvement. The need to bring in the state seemed to go against the ruling ideological conviction that not more but less state involvement was what was required. But many people changed their minds when the crisis struck.

In the twentieth century this conception of crisis as a prolonged political, economic and ideological impasse, for which political solutions had to be found, grew in importance. It owed its ascendancy in particular to the great crash of 1929 and the ensuing depression.

The Great Crash

The Great Depression of the 1930s began conventionally enough. There was a runaway boom in the 1920s which had increased prosperity to new heights in several countries, but particularly in the world's new leading economy, the United States. On the back of this the stock market had soared, and a speculative bubble in many different kinds of commodities and assets developed which rapidly got out of control. The crash, when it finally came in 1929, was spectacular, the greatest collapse of share prices ever recorded. It precipitated a major recession, but instead of this recession lasting the normal two years, it became a slump and a severe deflation. Prices in the United States dropped by a third and unemployment rose to

25 per cent of the workforce. Some estimates put it higher still. In Germany, output plunged and unemployment rose to six million. The American economy sunk into a depression from which it did not fully recover until the Second World War.

This was a capitalist crisis of a new type. There was no short, relatively brief crash and recession phase, no quick bounce back. The US economy fell into a deflationary hole from which it struggled to emerge. Most of the rest of the world struggled with it. The international monetary system fell apart with the collapse of the gold standard, with far-reaching political consequences for international trade and the international state system. With the spread of protectionism and currency blocs, world trade remained depressed, and the unified global economy of the period before 1914 was no more. Faced with this unprecedented economic downturn, there was widespread disagreement on its causes, and even more on the remedies. The split between Austrians and Keynesians came to the fore for the first time. It would not be the last. Much orthodox opinion in both Britain and the United States agreed with Hayek, that the slump needed to be even deeper if the conditions for recovery were to be restored. No artificial floor should be set by central banks or governments. Only if the bad debts, the bad investments and the bad loans were fully purged from the system could the ground be laid for a recovery. On the other side were those like Keynes who argued that new policies needed to be tried to kick start the economy and end the deflation. If the global economy could not be stabilized many countries would become ungovernable. Political leaders in those countries hardest hit, including the United States, with its New Deal programme, and Germany, with its big capital investment programme, began to experiment with new interventionist policies to get their economies moving again. In this way the intellectual halo around liberal political economy began to fade. Marxists and socialists had been persistent critics, but now even many of its friends began to concede that there needed to be a major rethink of economic policy.

Controversy has long reigned over why the crash turned into a depression and if it could have been avoided. The crash almost certainly could not have been prevented once a certain stage was reached. The bubble had just grown too big and when it burst the fallout was bound to be large. As in the 2008 crisis, there was extraordinary optimism expressed by financial leaders and political leaders right up to the end. President Coolidge declared in 1928, shortly before leaving office, that 'stocks are cheap at current prices' and he was echoed by many others. Even when the markets began to crash, there was widespread disbelief at first, and an expectation that this would turn out to be a minor setback, and that the market could rebound and go on to new heights. The stock market crash did not happen all at once. There were particularly bad days, like Black Thursday on 24 October 1929, but there were also significant rallies. What mattered was the trend in the market, which was remorselessly down. The worse year for stock market decline in prices was 1931, when the Dow lost 50 per cent of its value, still the worst year in the history of the index, although the present crash has begun to nudge towards it (in 2008 the Dow lost 38 per cent).

The big debate is whether the action of the authorities was appropriate. In general the authorities reacted in the classic manner – they refused to offer a general bailout to the banks. Firms that had got into trouble must accept the consequences. The market had to be allowed to take its course, so that true values could be established once more, and the moral integrity of the market upheld. The argument against intervention was an argument that was heard again in the 2008 crisis. If the markets perceive that the government will always bail out banks that get into difficulties, the banks have no incentive to be cautious in their lending. They will become irresponsible in their behaviour because they do not have to bear the consequences. This moral hazard was what the financial authorities in 1930 were most keen to avoid, and they did avoid it, but with rather spectacular consequences. In the United States the Federal Reserve tightened the supply of money rather than loosening it, and four thousand banks across the United States went to the wall, with huge consequences for businesses and households. Prices and wages fell, by up to one third in some cases, and unemployment and bankruptcies soared. Unemployment was to reach 17 million.

What became apparent was that this crisis had a number of complex and interlocking features, economic, political and ideological, which made it very hard to unravel. It was a crisis of a new type. It brought forth a lot of new thinking and innovation in economic theory, in public policy and in ideological narratives.

The policy of the United States Government under Herbert Hoover has become notorious as the 'do-nothing' policy, and it was widely condemned. But Hoover *was* doing something, he was following the conventional wisdom of the time about how to deal with a crash and a recession. He preferred not to see it as a crisis. No matter how severe the downturn, the recovery would come, so long as government did not get in the way and prevent the healing processes of the market from working.

The critics of the Hoover administration, both Keynesians and monetarists, have since argued that there were alternatives which should have been taken, and if they had been the slump could have been averted or would have been much shorter and more limited in its effects. There is fairly universal agreement among the critics that the Federal Reserve should have pursued a much more active monetary policy, although Keynesians have always argued that monetary policy alone would have been insufficient, and this has been echoed in the work of some recent sceptics, such as Peter Temin, who has argued that the decline in the money supply was not the cause of the downturn but the effect.

The case for it being the cause was made most strongly by Milton Friedman and Anna Schwarz in their study of the Great Depression. Milton Friedman, an academic economist in Chicago, rose to prominence in the 1960s as the leading protagonist of monetarism as the best theory for understanding how the macro-economy worked and for managing it. Schwarz and he argued that the depression was caused by the Federal Reserve contracting the money supply when it should have increased it. It was regulatory error. Had the Fed been alive to the serious risk of deflation it would have flooded the markets with liquidity in a bid to stave it off. Central bankers have taken the lesson to heart. Ben Bernanke, the current chairman of the Federal Reserve, even declared at a dinner on the occasion of Milton Friedman's ninetieth birthday: 'I would like to say to Milton and Anna. Regarding the Great Depression. You're right, we did it. We're very sorry. But thanks to you, we won't do it again.' It was fitting that it should be Ben Bernanke, keen student of the Great Depression, who should find himself in charge of the Federal Reserve in 2007–8, facing a new financial crash of the sort few had expected to see again. He had the opportunity he must never have expected – to put his theories about how to avoid deflation to the test. So far the evidence is mixed.

One lesson that Friedman, Bernanke and many others took from the Great Depression was that never again must central banks contract the money supply in response to a major crash and risk a major deflationary spiral. Whatever the moral hazard, the short-term policy had to be to flood the market with liquidity to prevent as many banks and other companies as possible from going out of business. The task of the Federal Reserve if such a crisis were to hit again must be to keep the financial system from seizing up, to do what it could to preserve trust and confidence. If the collapse in the financial markets could be moderated, then there might be a chance of preventing serious damage to the rest of the economy, and of a short recession and an early resumption of growth. This view assumed that the basic problem was a monetary one, and needed a monetary solution.

John Maynard Keynes, Cambridge economist and an adviser to the British Treasury during both world wars, had approached the problem during the 1930s from a different angle. For him the main cause of the slump and the depression lay with the real economy rather than the monetary economy, and he argued that direct fiscal measures to stimulate demand and redistribute income and spending power were required. The situation was exacerbated by the working of financial markets in modern capitalism which constantly tended to instability and to create liquidity traps, preventing money being used where it might actually create jobs. Left alone, a market economy could settle down with prolonged underemployment of resources. The existence of radical uncertainty and limited knowledge on the part of market agents meant that the economic structure of modern capitalism was highly fragile, and that there was no spontaneous tendency for the economy to move to full employment. It could be stuck in a liquidity trap for years. Keynes argued that new thinking was needed to deal with a new economic situation. Government had to be ready to take a much bigger role and assume responsibility for stabilizing demand and managing the economy. Friedman believed that the interventions by the authorities, while necessary, should be strictly limited and temporary, and confined to monetary measures. Once the rescue had been performed, the market would regulate itself again. Keynes believed that financial instability was a permanent feature of modern capitalism, and would require government intervention if there was to be sustained full employment, and that the government had to be ready to use both monetary and fiscal measures. He set about rewriting economics to show how this was the case theoretically, but his basic insight was a practical one, derived from observing how the markets actually performed and witnessing at first hand the catastrophe of the slump and the depression. He warned strongly against the danger of deflation in modern economies, the possibility of liquidity traps and the difficulty of economies recovering on their own. If there had to be a choice between inflation and deflation he opted for the former. The right remedy for the trade cycle, he wrote, 'is not to be found in abolishing booms and thus keeping us permanently in a semi-slump; but in abolishing slumps and thus keeping us permanently in a quasi-boom' (Keynes, 1973, pp. 321–2).

Keynesianism was developed in a number of directions by Keynes' followers in the 1950s and 1960s, and only a few continued to be interested in his monetary theories and the contribution of financial markets to the instability of capitalist economies and the business cycle. An exception was Hyman Minsky, an economist based at St Louis, Missouri, who developed a theory which he called 'the financial instability hypothesis'. It developed some of the insights of Keynes and earlier economists into the workings of the financial markets, and how because these markets were qualitatively different from other markets under capitalism they could not be analysed in the same way. Minsky suggested, in the 1970s, that there was an inherent tendency for financial markets to create speculative investment bubbles, and to become disconnected from the real economy, swinging between robustness and fragility. The idea that financial markets were 'efficient' or 'optimal' in some sense was alien to him. The only way to control this inherent instability was through government intervention and regulation, the kind of policies that were introduced by the Roosevelt administration in the 1930s, such as the enforced separation of retail and investment banking, and reform of corporate governance. These reforms lasted until they were dismantled in the 1980s and 1990s in deference to the new financial growth model, and the euphoria that accompanied the boom.

Other Keynesians focused less on the monetary economy than on the real economy. For John Kenneth Galbraith, who had served in the US Government during the Second World War and afterwards held an economics chair at Harvard, it was structural weaknesses in the US economy that turned the slump into a depression, among them the inequality of incomes in the US, which limited the purchasing power of the lower income groups, and the growth of protectionism. Both these factors were highlighted by many other historians and economists. In a seminal study, Charles Kindleberger, Professor of Economics at MIT, argued that the basic cause of the depression was the breakdown in the international financial system and in the broader structures for governing the world economy. The failure of the 1930s was that no state took on the role of hegemon for the global economy and created the policies and institutions needed to stabilize it. Britain had the will to perform this role but no longer had the capacity, while the United States had the capacity, but did not yet possess the will. The foundering of the global economy and the growth of protectionism meant that economic recovery had to be organized nation by nation, which proved much less successful than a reorganized international system might have been. The way in which the crisis had been constructed politically at the time, in the 1930s, as a national problem requiring national responses and national remedies, looked inadequate from this perspective. It was to have a major impact on thinking during the 1970s crisis.

These analyses looked beyond just monetary or economic policy to the political conditions necessary to promote a general recovery. The degree of interconnectedness of the world economy, and the much larger role for the state which had emerged, gave a new meaning to capitalist crisis. Downturns could not be treated any longer as a natural process within the workings of the capitalist business cycle, which if left alone would produce their own corrective mechanism. What were needed were more far-reaching political and economic changes in order to create the conditions for a new burst of accumulation. The obstacles that had to be removed were not just prices and wages that were too high, and companies that were no longer efficient, but also political and social institutions that made it difficult to reduce prices sufficiently, and blocked the development of trade. The problems were not just national but international, and this required international solutions, but there was no sovereign power to impose them; mechanisms had to be found for gaining the consent of the most important economic players. The global character both of the crisis and of the solutions to it became one of the main conclusions from retrospective assessments of the 1930s.

The 1970s Stagflation

The Great Depression did prove to be a watershed in the history of capitalism, not least because it changed the understanding of what was involved in a capitalist crisis, and what remedies were available to deal with it. The catastrophe that overwhelmed first the global economy and then the international state system in the 1930s, plunging the world at the end of the decade into the Second World War, left a deep imprint, and a resolve that it should never be allowed to happen again. The state everywhere became much more active and interventionist, and fundamental social reforms were agreed that changed the face of capitalism in many countries. Capitalism after 1950, when the new upswing started, was very different from what it had been. Many of the national protectionist features that had become prominent in the 1930s survived but in an attenuated form, and the general trend was towards their removal. The reconstitution of a liberal global economy and the international monetary system under American leadership created once more the conditions for the growth of trade, investment and interdependence, and this succeeded beyond expectations in the 1950s and 1960s, with capitalism recording its most successful period of progress.

Capitalism was, however, now viewed in a different way. The various regulatory reforms which had been enacted, the big extension of state powers, the new emphasis on welfare, the creation of a mixed economy, all contributed to the idea that capitalist crisis would never be the same again. There would still be booms and recessions, but governments now knew enough to prevent those recessions turning into long-lasting depressions. The price, it was conceded, was permanent inflation, but here again governments thought they could manage it. Low rates of inflation were not a serious problem and even stimulated growth by rewarding debtors and penalizing creditors. Few believed there could be a return to the principles of sound finance, putting financial stability ahead of all other considerations. Governments had baulked at the severity of the price and wage cuts that would have been needed to restore financial discipline in the wake of the Great Depression, and they were not disposed to try it now. In this way, the long inflationary boom was born. Andrew Shonfield, writing in the 1960s, declared that the fluctuations of the capitalist business cycle were now so mild that the terms once used to describe it were no longer relevant. This was not the cycle that the Austrians had praised and the Marxists had condemned. The basic financial disciplines had been removed, but this had not undermined capitalism, it seemed to have strengthened it. Capitalism no longer seemed prone to the violent oscillations of the old business cycle. This was managed capitalism. Many Marxists accepted as much and wrote detailed analyses of how capitalism had fundamentally changed, and was no longer subject to the old kind of crisis.

Those Austrians and orthodox Marxists who remained attached to the older meaning of crisis, as a necessary part of a self-regulating economic mechanism which governments could not interfere with, were keen to insist that this Keynesian idyll would not last, and that it would undermine its own foundations. Hayek predicted that the inflationary boom would eventually destroy itself and that there would have, at some time, to be a return to capitalist fundamentals. He feared that this might be very difficult and painful to accomplish, so corroded had the institutions of a free society become by decades of state intervention and collectivist welfare. But a reckoning there would have to be if capitalism was to survive. Hayek and many others in the free market think tanks began to develop narratives as to why the Keynesian welfare state was bound to end in disaster, because of its inability to survive except by increasing inflation, and by its tendency to expand the state and increase taxation and other burdens on individuals and enterprises.

Marxists in the 1960s developed two lines of argument against the ruling discourse of the welfare state and the mixed economy, which Keynesianism promoted. The first was that capitalist crisis needed to be re-evaluated. The ten-year business cycle of the nineteenth century was a specific historical pattern which belonged to a particular period. The conditions for it had now disappeared. What still existed, however, were much longer cycles, the so-called long waves, which the Russian economist Kondratieff had described in the 1920s. These long waves might last between fifty and sixty years, and could contain within them many shorter cycles. In the first part of the cycle growth tended to be much stronger; in the second half it tended to be much weaker. These cycles were made possible by the bunching of a number of major innovations which did not just transform production in a single industry, but had a broad effect on a wide range of industries throughout the economy. They involved not just the introduction of new products and methods of production, but new markets and new forms of organization. The working through of all the implications of one of these fundamental technologies, like electricity, or the internal combustion engine, provided the spur for very strong growth, and as the possibilities became exhausted so the possibilities declined. The importance of this theory of long waves was that it allowed the history of capitalism to be understood as a succession of great leaps forward, followed by periods in which growth declined, and punctuated by periods of economic and political crisis, in which many relations had to be transformed before a new growth spurt could occur. In the hands of some of its theorists, long wave theory suggested that this task of reconstructing the basis for the next period of successful capitalist advance grew steadily more difficult with each succeeding cycle, although not impossible. The Great Depression assumed a special place in the later theories of the long wave because its occurrence seemed to validate Kondratieff's account, and suggested that the enormous political and economic upheavals of the 1930s had been necessary to provide the conditions for the great capitalist boom after 1945. But if Kondratieff was correct this boom was sure to wind down eventually and lead to another period of turmoil and upheaval. It would produce a crisis which governments would not be able to control or manage in the way they had been able to manage the much smaller problem of smoothing out the economic cycle during the years of the boom.

Other Marxists rejected long wave theory as overly determinist, and focused more on the changed nature of capitalism, arguing that Keynesian techniques for managing demand, the new forms of regulation, much higher levels of government spending, the welfare state and citizenship rights, meant that while capitalism had not got rid of all its problems it was not going to face the kind of breakdown through economic crisis that had been predicted and confidently expected for so long. The 1930s was that crisis, and yet capitalism had not only survived, but also had eventually emerged much stronger, and much better equipped to deal with crises in the future. By intervening in the market governments had reconstructed capitalism on a new basis. This was a capitalism in which many of the old ills of capitalism were less in evidence, and in which there were prospects for workers to achieve higher standards of living and much greater economic security. The technical capacities of governments to control the capitalist cycle and mitigate its worst effects meant that socialists could no longer expect economic crisis to make capitalism unsustainable. Jurgen Habermas, one of the last representatives of the Frankfurt school, argued that if capitalism still faced a crisis, it was no longer an economic crisis. The steering capacities of the state were now sufficient to postpone or defuse such potential for crisis indefinitely. The crisis was now different, it was a crisis of legitimation, because for all their technical mastery, governments found it hard to deliver what their citizens wanted or to make the management of the economy legitimate, except through encouraging ever greater consumption, ever greater credit and debt, and ever greater material satisfactions. Schumpeter might well have agreed, although he would have said it was the price that had to be paid for the triumph of socialism and bureaucracy and the end of the kind of entrepreneurial and moral capitalism which he favoured.

Habermas was important in the history of thinking about crisis in another way, because he pioneered ways of thinking about crises as political events which arose because the dominant interpretations of political reality were no longer accepted. The heart of the crisis was the challenge to established power, the denial of its legitimacy and the bid to offer different interpretations. He developed his theory of legitimation crisis in response to the second major capitalist crisis of the twentieth century, the 1970s stagflation. This was a crisis on a lesser scale than the 1930s, but it was still responsible for some major changes in the structure of the economy, in international and national politics, and in dominant ideologies. It confounded some of the easy optimism which had been building through the 1950s and 1960s that capitalism was no longer generating serious problems. At the same time it confirmed the much greater capacity governments had acquired to respond to economic challenges and ride out crises. Some major shifts of policy took place, and the birth of a new policy regime and ideological discourse, but the upheaval was limited. The first global recession since 1945 was handled reasonably successfully. It made necessary some painful restructuring but governments were proactive rather than reactive. Many different solutions to the crisis were canvassed and political positions polarized. It was an authentic moment of danger, and there were some dramatic confrontations in several countries. It was the first visible check to the unquestioned dominance of the United States in governing the global economy. The dollar continued as the main international reserve currency, and the US as the dominant economic and financial power, but the US abandoned the fixed exchange rate system, and sought to maintain its dominance by crafting a different kind of order, one less predictable and inherently more fragile, resting as it did on the expansion of the financial markets as a leading sector.

These events gave comfort to those like Hayek who had argued that eventually Keynesianism would be discredited, and that a new policy regime would have to be installed to tackle inflation. This certainly occurred, and was one of the most obvious outcomes of the 1970s crisis. But the state remained a very powerful actor. Despite some of the rhetoric there was no real attempt to roll back the state, or seriously curtail its role. The crisis was still politically managed, there was no question of governments standing back and allowing the market itself to sort it out. If anything, during the neo-liberal era the state became still more deeply involved in attempts to reform the public sector and create conditions for growth in the wider economy. Even the deregulation that occurred was more than it seemed. Often it involved re-regulation, the transference of regulatory powers to new bodies, or the setting up of new regulatory agencies. The neo-liberal state was a regulatory state, not a laissez-faire state.

The crisis in the 1970s was severe enough and complicated enough for long wave theorists to recognize it as a significant event in the long period of expansion that had begun in the years after 1945, but if their estimate of the length of long waves was correct, then this crisis could not be the crisis at the end of the long wave, but only one in the middle. There was still a further up-phase of the long wave, the secondary plateau, to come. Depending on when the start of the up wave was dated, the next contractionary phase was not due until early in the twenty-first century. On this view the crisis of the 1970s was only a staging post. It allowed a reconfiguring of the post-war coordinates of global capitalism which made possible a second boom, less powerful than the first in the 1950s and 1960s, but still substantial. It was this boom starting in the 1980s and gathering strength through the 1990s which came to a definitive end in 2008. Long wave theory has many critics, because it always seems to involve some stretching of the evidence. But it retains a degree of plausibility if only because in the industrial era there has been a certain rhythm to economic development, which since 1930 has produced so far two major contractionary phases and two major booms. Now a new contractionary phase has begun, but beyond it, if long wave theory is correct, lies a major new up wave, if we can just get there. But such patterns can be deceptive, and the existence of such patterns in the past is no guarantee they will be repeated in the future.

It is impossible to be sure as yet about the magnitude of the change which the events of 2007–8 portend, and analogies from the past can be misleading if pressed too far. But just as the 1930s and the 1970s have come to be seen in retrospect as major turning points in the way in which the global economy and its governance developed, so 2008 and 2009 may well come to be seen as another such turning point. Many of the events have been as dramatic as any that took place in the early stages of the crises in 1929–31 and 1973–5, and there is much more to come.

Explanations of 2008 are still in their infancy. But many of the old tunes are still with us. There has been much pointing at the evidence once again of human greed and folly in contributing to this man-made catastrophe. There are Austrian and Marxist accounts which find vindication once again for their long-held beliefs in the inner laws which drive capitalism. There is vindication too for the theories of Keynes and Minsky, for the acuteness with which they analysed the way financial markets actually work under capitalism, and how the deregulation promoted in the 1980s and 1990s ignored many of those insights. There is a certain symmetry in the rise and fall of theories. After the Great Depression there was the rise of what might be called 'the efficient government thesis', the belief that government could acquire enough knowledge and enough capacity to manage capitalism successfully and smooth out the fluctuations of the capitalist trade cycle. After the 1970s stagflation had so damaged that thesis, a new thesis arose in its place. This was the 'efficient markets thesis', the belief that markets if left alone would always price assets correctly. After the events of 2007–8 the efficient markets thesis is in ruins, and the world is due for a new intellectual and policy revolution. Whether it will get it is not so clear.

3
Globalization and Neo-liberalism

The last two periods of capitalist crisis, in the 1930s and the 1970s, gave rise to major ideological as well as political and economic shifts. New ideas became important both in framing the crisis and determining what kind of crisis it was, and what solutions were appropriate. The way in which certain events come to be perceived as a crisis is always complex and always a political act, since it authorizes certain courses of action to resolve the crisis and restore stability or create a new order. New ideas, or perhaps the return of some old ones, will also be vitally important in determining how the present crisis is understood and resolved. As discussed in the last chaper, to call any set of events or circumstances a crisis suggests either that there is a critical situation, a political emergency, a moment of danger, or that an impasse of some kind has been reached. In either case, extraordinary actions may be required to overcome it.

This chapter explores the rise of two powerful sets of ideas, globalization and neo-liberalism, out of the crisis of the 1970s. For almost thirty years they have ruled virtually unchallenged. It asks whether this era came to an end in 2008 and 2009, just as the 1970s crisis brought the Keynesian era to an end. There was nothing inevitable about the triumph of neo-liberalism; a number of political, economic and ideological interventions and circumstances combined to make it possible. The post-war consensus on economic management had seemed solid. The remarkable stabilization of capitalism at both global and national levels which had taken place in the 1950s and 1960s had produced an exceptional era of prosperity and economic advance in the capitalist heartlands. But this was now challenged by a novel set of economic and political problems – the collapse of the fixed exchange rate system that had held for twenty-five years; an acceleration of inflation coinciding with a marked slowdown in economic growth; an explosion of commodity prices, particularly oil; an upsurge of strikes; and restiveness on the capitalist periphery with the exploration of alternative and non-capitalist paths of development by several countries. These mounting difficulties caused an abrupt change of mood. As the crisis deepened and the world plunged into the first major global recession of the postwar era, much of the confidence of the previous two decades was lost too.

In the 1950s the end of ideology had been celebrated in the West, reflecting the triumph of one particular version of the western ideology. There was a broad consensus on the new hybrid forms of capitalism that had emerged, with their emphasis on economic management and high state expenditure. During the 1970s stagflation, ideological debate returned with some force, and the basis of the political settlement between labour and capital, the 'Keynesian welfare state', which had stabilized and legitimized capitalism since the 1940s, came under challenge. Keynesianism and the welfare state had become linked together because of the belief that without full employment the creation of universal and comprehensive welfare programmes which offered protection from the cradle to the grave could not be afforded. The way to guarantee full employment was to use the techniques of Keynesian demand management, controlling the business cycles of the capitalist economy and avoiding deep recessions through a mix of fiscal and monetary policies.

The growing inability of governments to manage the capitalist business cycle, mild though it was in the first two decades after the Second World War, and above all their failure to control inflation, was one of the main causes of renewed political polarization, and the reopening of a fresh divide on economic policy on traditional left/right lines, with the left favouring state solutions to the crisis and the right market solutions. Many on the left expected that this new capitalist crisis would create strategic openings for anti-capitalist forces of all kinds, both in the advanced economies and in the Global South. But the crisis also created strategic openings on the right, and the right generally proved more adept at seizing them. The 1970s and 1980s produced a great convulsion in world capitalism, at once economic, political and ideological, and a period of heightened change in the familiar landmarks of all three. One of the most significant features of this period was the revival of doctrines of the free market, both as ideology and as political economy. Neo-liberalism constructed one of the most successful and influential depictions of the events of the 1970s, labelling them a crisis of social democracy, of Keynesianism and of the extended state which it claimed the first two had brought into being and which were now stifling the market economy.

There was disagreement at first among those who were attacked as to what the emergence of neo-liberal ideology meant, and whether it represented a new course or an attempt to return to an old one. At first it was rejected for trying to put the clock back to an era of capitalism which no longer existed, the liberal capitalism of the nineteenth century. But this was never accurate. Neo-liberalism was indeed new, as the prefix 'neo' implied, and was to play an integral part in the far-reaching reorganization of state and economy which took place in response to the 1970s stagflation. Its genesis is explored below.

Globalization

Neo-liberalism would not have attained the ascendancy it did without globalization. Globalization needs to be understood in two ways, both as a set of processes which it is often claimed are gradually creating an integrated global economy, and as a particular ideological discourse about those processes. The ways in which the world order was reconstructed in the 1970s and 1980s put in place the conditions for a new period of growth, and gave impetus to the various trends and processes which became known as globalization. The idea of globalization took off in the 1980s and became irresistible in the 1990s, once the Soviet Union had fallen, and so the possibility of a reunification of the world economy as one system, one global economy, had been restored.

A distinction needs to be made between the academic study of globalization and the popular discourse of globalization. The academic study focuses on the question of how far the world economy moved in the 1980s and 1990s to become a unified global economy, and how far it remained an international economy with national and regional foundations. This debate is between those who take a 'transformationalist' perspective, and their critics. The transformationalists argue that the processes of globalization have had real effects in many different areas, including industrial production, in finance, in communications, in technology, in commerce and in culture, and are steadily transforming the international economy into an interconnected global economy even if the process is highly uneven and incomplete. The critics point to all the ways in which the economy is not truly global and in certain respects can be regarded as less global than before 1914. They object to using the term global economy at all because it implies a degree of integration which they argue does not exist and is therefore misleading. This debate has been one of the most important in contemporary social science, and it has done a great deal to clarify the nature and direction of recent economic and political change.

Running parallel to this debate, but largely separate from it, has been the discourse of globalization that has been popularized in the media and by some business schools, and has gripped the imagination of many in the political class across the world. This discourse, best described as hyper-globalization, and the discourse of neo-liberalism fed one another from the outset. Hyper-globalists, such as Kenichi Ohmae, have argued that the era of national protectionism which had lasted more or less continuously since the First World War is now over, and that this means that the state has once again become subordinate to the market, in the way that it had been in the nineteenth century. They proclaimed the end of the nation state, and the creation of a borderless world, through the breaking down of national boundaries by the rise of economic forces which simply bypassed them. The image this hyper-globalization discourse created was of a world which was integrating economically very fast, in which connections of all kinds between societies, but especially economic ones, were multiplying, and in the face of which the traditional powers and capacities of states were increasingly inadequate to cope. As evidence they pointed to the power of multinational companies to organize and site production where they wished, forcing national governments to accommodate them, and also to the power of the financial markets, able to dispose of such financial power (transactions worth $1 trillion dollars a day) that they could break any government or central bank which lost their confidence.

Neo-liberals applauded the triumph of markets over governments which the hyper-globalists described. Runs on a currency could destabilize a government and force it to borrow from the IMF, as Britain had to do in 1976. The price of being bailed out was accepting neo-liberal constraints on the policies that could be followed. Governments that wanted to spend to protect their citizens from the effects of the recession found that they could not do so if they lost the confidence of the financial markets. The speed with which capital could flee an economy provided severe constraints on what governments could do. During Francois Mitterrand's first term as French President the government had to change course in 1983, abandon its socialist and Keynesian economic programme and announce the 'liberal turn' in its economic policy, because of pressure on the franc. Sweden, in 1992, had to abandon the defence of its exchange rate and announce major changes in economic policy, including the national-ization of its banks. States learned that 'You cannot buck the markets', a phrase popularized by Margaret Thatcher. It became one of the slogans of neo-liberalism, and it came straight from the discourse of the hyper-globalists, a recognition of the new power of the financial markets. In the neo-liberal era all governments found they had to accommodate to this power of the financial markets and adopt policies which would not disturb international financial confidence.

The global financial crash of 2008 did not just prick the asset bubbles of the financial markets. It also burst the ideological bubble of neo-liberalism which had been inflating for three decades, and cast doubt on the claims of the hyper-globalists. To adapt Hayek, it was time to shout from the house-tops that the intellectual foundations of neo-liberalism had all collapsed. Many took the opportunity to do so. Yet how badly damaged neo-liberalism will be by the financial crash of 2008 and the recession of 2009 remains to be seen. As an ideology it has strong recuperative powers, and neo-liberals will almost certainly try to regroup, and turn the crisis to their advantage. They are already seeking to develop their own narrative of the crash and what caused it, arguing that the crisis has been caused by failures of regulation rather than failures of markets. Neo-liberals hope by this means to seize back the ground they have lost and start setting the agenda once more. But, like Keynesianism in the 1970s, neo-liberalism has suffered some hammer blows, particularly as a result of the dethronement and in some places the defenestration of finance, and has temporarily lost its bearings.

It already seems a while since the glad, confident morning of neo-liberalism, and the emergence of neo-liberalism as the new common sense. It had a hard fight against the 'embedded liberalism' of the Keynesian era, the combination of international institutions, such as fixed exchange rates, and domestic policies, such as full employment, high welfare spending, and management of demand, which underpinned the great post-war boom of the 1950s and 1960s. But once neo-liberalism got into its stride it became a formidable discourse, and dominated debate, forcing most other discourses to the margins, particularly in the Anglosphere but also more broadly. Its success owed much to its reinvention of economic liberalism both as a form of political economy and as a political ideology. Like any discourse, it was never monolithic and developed many strands, but by the end of the century it was not just a hegemonic ideology but a largely unchallenged one. This came about because of the collapse of communism in the USSR and in east and central Europe, the pro-market turn of China and the fading of alternative paths of development in the Third World. There were still pockets of resistance, particularly in western social democracy, and in parts of the Global South and the Middle East. But even here countries and regimes were obliged to come to terms with the new order. Capital was everywhere triumphant, and the old simplicities of economic liberalism were being expressed once more as unremarkable common sense. By 2000 they were encountering relatively little challenge, either politically or intellectually. The world was once again proclaimed to be One World, and it was a neo-liberal world.

Things looked very different in 2008, and some began to seriously doubt whether neo-liberalism could recover as a ruling set of ideas, or whether it was doomed like the banks. There was certainly no shortage of attempts by neo-liberals to explain away what had happened in the financial markets as all the fault of government and of too much regulation rather than too little. But many had stopped listening. Neo-liberalism seemed implicated up to the hilt in what had happened in the previous two decades and what had gone wrong. At the very least the prospect of a substantial downgrading of the importance of finance and the scale of its activities in many national economies, as well as much tighter regulation both nationally and internationally, were widely anticipated as the minimum changes that would be needed. To a great extent the fate of neo-liberalism had come to rest on the future of the global economy, whether its relative openness could be preserved, or whether it would relapse into closed regionalism and protectionism. To survive neo-liberalism needs the trends towards a more integrated global economy to continue, and it needs the financial sector to regain its position as an important element in the global economy. If the trend towards financial protectionism which became evident in 2008 was to become established, with banks in each country increasingly unwilling to lend to banks in other countries, the consequences could be as serious as trade protectionism. Neo-liberalism in one country would in practical terms be as doomed as socialism in one country turned out to be.

Neo-liberalism

Neo-liberalism is not a term much used by many of those who have the label attached to them. Many neo-liberals prefer to call themselves free market liberals, classical liberals, liberal conservatives, economic conservatives or simply plain economic liberals. But there is enough that is new about these economic liberals to retain the term. It was first used in the 1930s in a very different context, by the German economist Alexander

Rüstow, to describe new currents of liberal thought which were hostile to the forms of statism and collectivism which had been so dominant in the first few decades of the twentieth century. Rüstow sought a new form of political economy which would give priority to market rather than bureaucratic or hierarchical means of ordering the economy, within a framework of law. This attempt to go back to first principles and refound economic liberalism was an important inspiration for the experiments with a social market economy in Germany after 1945, and also was part of the movement that led to the founding of the Mont Pelerin society in 1948 by Hayek, Friedman and other leading economic liberals. The Mont Pelerin society stood for the reassertion of classical liberal principles in a world that its participants saw as dominated by anti-liberal ideals, from the communism of the Soviet Union to the social democracy of Europe and the programme of the New Deal in the United States. Mont Pelerin was primarily a discussion circle for intellectuals, but many of its members were to be key figures in the later dissemination and popularization of neo-liberal ideas.

There has never been one neo-liberalism. There have always been a number of strands within this increasingly influential discourse, many of which reflect aspects of classical liberalism in the nineteenth century. There is a laissez-faire strand, often now labelled market fundamentalism, which believes that markets should be allowed to function with as few impediments as possible; there is an anarcho-capitalist strand which seeks the privatization of all state functions, including defence, law enforcement and all forms of economic and financial regulation; and there is a social market strand, which believes that for the free market to reach its full potential the state has to be active in creating and sustaining the institutions that make that possible. Anarcho-capitalism is something of an outlier in policy debate, although its radicalism has always exerted a fascination for the neo-liberal persuasion. The other two strands give priority to the market within social relations, and both imply an active state. But for laissez-faire neo-liberals the role of the state is primarily to remove obstacles to the way markets function, while for social market neo-liberals the state also has a responsibility to intervene to create the right kind of institutional setting within which markets can function. This second strand of neo-liberalism legitimates a wide range of state intervention – from the encouragement of structural adjustment, social capital and good governance in developing economies, to welfare safety nets, to investment in human capital, to environmental protection, to corporate social responsibility, even to limited forms of redistribution. The laissez-faire strand, by contrast, is more hardheaded and minimalist. It is much more averse to any kind of interference with markets by governments, believing that such interventions do more harm than good, and that the outcomes of markets left to themselves are almost always benign, or at least as benign as it is possible for outcomes to be in an imperfect world. The efficient markets hypothesis is a typical product of this strand. It holds that markets left to themselves will always tend to produce the most optimal outcomes, and certainly more optimal outcomes than the most well-informed and well-intentioned regulation can ever achieve.

It might be better if the label neo-liberalism had been confined to the laissez-faire strand (even then it would be fairly broad), but this would exclude many ideas and policies which are routinely dubbed 'neo-liberal' in many different regions around the world – the policies of many international agencies for example, including the World Bank and the IMF, as well as governments of different party complexions. Neo-liberalism, like many other ideologies, is made up of contradictory ideas and principles which are used quite freely to construct a range of different discourses. Nevertheless there do remain some core ideas by which all strands of neo-liberalism are recognizable, and one of these is the relationship of the state to the market. For neo-liberals the market has primacy, but at the same time they recognize that a market order needs a particular kind of state to secure it. A free economy requires a strong state, both to overcome the obstacles and resistance to the institutions of a free economy, which constantly recur, and also to provide the non-market institutions, which are necessary for the market to be successful and legitimate. The necessity for the economy to be free and the state to be strong is perhaps the chief hallmark of neo-liberal thinking, but also one of the main sources of its contradictions, and one of the main sources of its internal debates. Neo-liberals do not agree among themselves in which areas of state activity the state should be strong and where the line should be drawn. Some want it to be very limited indeed; others argue for a larger role for state action, particularly in periods of crisis. A recent example has been the debates over how to respond to the financial crash in 2008. Pragmatists have supported extensive bank bailouts, even bank nationalizations, so long as these are temporary, while fundamentalists have opposed the state becoming involved, arguing that these things are best left to the market to sort out.

As an intellectual doctrine neo-liberalism was influential in Germany in the 1950s, but first began to acquire wider attention through the critique of

Keynesianism that was mounted in the Anglo-American world in the late 1960s by a number of economists and think tanks, including the Institute of Economic Affairs in London and the American Enterprise Institute in Washington. Critics of Keynesianism had never gone away; there had always been an undercurrent of dissent, both in the academy and in the political world, but this had largely been silenced by the enormous success of the post-war economy, even if little of this was directly attributable to Keynesianism. The specific Keynesian remedies against depression had not been needed in the 1950s and 1960s. The problem was not too little demand, but too much. Governments had adapted Keynesian ideas to deal with an economy that continually threatened to overheat, using fiscal measures to fine tune demand. In retrospect both inflation and unemployment were remarkably low, and the economic problems that existed were relatively minor. There was, however, a persistent upward creep of inflation, which began to produce interventions aimed at controlling prices and wages. These incomes policies had nothing to do with classical Keynesianism, but they were seen as being in the spirit of Keynesianism, with its preference for using the state to sort out the problems in the markets.

The rise in inflation and the ineffectiveness of government policies aimed at reducing it gave the neo-liberals their opportunity. The spearhead of the attack was the doctrine of monetarism formulated by a number of economists, including Milton Friedman, David Laidler and Karl Brunner. Monetarism as a macro-economic doctrine still owed much to Keynes, and might even be labelled monetary Keynesianism, since what it chiefly opposed was the fiscal Keynesianism of the 1950s and 1960s, which had tried to fine tune demand, and in the view of monetarists had led to attempts to control wages and prices, and to direct economic growth and trade. By the end of the 1960s Keynesian political economy had lost its former connection with monetary policy, and this created the space for the monetarist counter-revolution.

The significance of monetarism was that it became much more than just an intellectual riposte to Keynesian support for using fiscal instruments to manage demand. Monetarism provided an intellectual bridgehead which allowed a much wider hearing for the critique of state involvement in the economy associated with other currents of neo-liberal thought, such as the Austrian school in which Friedrich Hayek and Ludwig von Mises were still prominent, the Virginia school of public choice around James Buchanan and assorted economic liberals, libertarians and anarcho-capi- talists. By the early 1970s the writings and key ideas of Friedman, Hayek and other prominent neo-liberals were being widely disseminated by neo-liberal and conservative think tanks in both Britain and the United States, and by the comment columns in key newspapers which reached the political class, such as the *Financial Times* in London and *The Wall Street Journal* in New York.

The acceleration of inflation in the leading capitalist economies at the end of the 1960s allowed the monetarist critique of Keynesianism to open the door to an anti-Keynesian political economy. Before then the policy position associated with the Austrian School critique of social democracy had often been regarded as purely 'ideological' in a pejorative sense, having no real purchase on the realities of modern capitalism. When Hayek's *The Constitution of Liberty* had appeared in 1960 it was described by George Lichtheim as advocating a return to nineteenth-century laissez-faire, something which he regarded not only as undesirable but as impractical:

> With its remorseless extrapolation of the logic inherent in the liberal doctrine, its unflinching demonstration that individualism is incompatible with the vital needs of modern society, this massive work stands as both a timely waning to political philosophers and an impressive monument to a myth. (1960, p. 107)

Capitalism was now corporate capitalism, as Galbraith among others never ceased to point out. It required very different ways of legitimating and organizing itself than the simple precepts of economic liberalism allowed. Keynesians were inclined to think that the basis of capitalism's post-war success was due in great measure to the role now played by the state in building prosperous national economies and redistributive welfare states, and actively promoting development and modernization around the globe. Whether recovering from the Depression of the 1930s, rebuilding a new economy and social order after 1945, or projecting a development model, a blueprint for modernization for the whole world, the state after 1945 had a role at least equal to that of the market, and in many instances a role superior to it. The idea that the state should cease to be interventionist and should revert to a nineteenth-century 'nightwatchman' role, unlearning the lessons of Keynesianism and of social democracy and planned development, seemed likely to precipitate a much deeper crisis for capitalism than the one that was currently being faced.

Keynesianism, like neo-liberalism, had its greatest influence and found its strongest advocates in Britain and the United States, but the assumptions about the nature of the economy and the role of the state which informed it were part of a much wider movement of thought and policy, which found expression in the social democracy of many European countries, as well as the developmental state of Japan. Andrew Shonfield's account of *Modern Capitalism*, written in the 1960s, drew attention to the ubiquitous involvement of the state in managing the economy in contemporary capitalist societies, regardless of the ideology or the economic doctrines professed by the different governments. The extent of state involvement still varied, and in some countries, notably Germany, it was more limited than in others, but Shonfield was able to demonstrate that in all of the advanced capitalist economies the state was now expected to play an active role and had developed the institutional capacities to do so.

What was surprising, given the intellectual and political self-confidence of the Keynesian generation, was the speed with which the ideas of neo-liberalism jumped the barrier into practical politics, establishing themselves as the leading ideas both in the national politics of particular states and, perhaps more crucially, in the thinking of the international agencies of the global order such as the IMF and the World Bank in the 1970s and 1980s. If neo-liberalism had had to rely for its dissemination on the internal politics of each individual capitalist state, its spread and its influence might have been slower. But the decision by the United States in 1971 to abandon the fixed exchange rate system centred on the dollar and the floating of all the major currencies gave an enormous boost to monetarist ideas as the means for containing inflation from the mid-1970s onwards. Greater priority came to be given to monetary rather than fiscal policy instruments. The adoption of basic monetarist precepts by the international agencies as the new orthodoxy for containing the problems of stagflation was a crucial development. The translation of these ideas into domestic programmes in the United States, Canada, Australia, New Zealand and Britain followed, with consequent effects on the politics of all the other major economies in the OECD economies, including France, Germany and Japan, together with new international programmes for dealing with the escalating debt of many developing economies.

Capitalism was different after the 1970s. It entered a new phase, and neo-liberalism was crucial to it. Yet many analysts still insisted on seeing it as an aberration, a throwback to an earlier period of capitalism, a revival of the discredited doctrines of laissez-faire, lacking foundations in the contemporary capitalist world. They dismissed it as a serious response to the problems facing capitalism in the 1970s. There was a widespread assumption, for example, that modern capitalism could not afford the remedies offered by neo-liberalism. Modern capitalist economies were characterized by extended state sectors, multinational companies, international financial markets, mass consumer markets and democratic political institutions. If neo-liberal remedies were to be adopted the result would be economic disaster, precipitating collapse on the scale of the 1930s, and the eruption of major class struggles, and a huge spur to anti-capitalist movements in the capitalist periphery seeking to break away or insulate themselves from the global market.

At the domestic level, Keynesianism was still widely regarded as the most effective economic and political strategy for capitalism. It legitimated an active state to stabilize demand and maintain the economy close to full employment through the use of automatic stabilizers and high levels of public spending on welfare and defence programmes. Fiscal Keynesianism or some similar doctrine seemed perfectly attuned to the requirements of a mass production, mass consumption Fordist economy, which had been pioneered by the United States. A form of managed capitalism seemed to be required by the complexity of modern cities and economies. The state had to be ready to step in to support an orderly development of demand, and to correct deficiencies of supply. The Keynesian policy regime was in difficulties in the 1970s because of the acceleration of inflation which exacerbated the fiscal crisis of the state and precipitated recession and sharply rising unemployment. But many economists continued to think that the choice, as far as the advanced economies were concerned, was between a 'Keynesianism plus' programme, or some kind of socialist alternative. Keynesianism plus was being developed in a number of countries, particularly Sweden in the 1970s, and involved going beyond fiscal Keynesianism and indirect means of managing demand in the economy, and instead developing new institutions and policies to control investment decisions and implement radical measures of redistribution by giving workers direct shares in the profits of enterprises.

By the end of the 1980s, with a speed which was breathtaking, neo-liberalism had successfully redrawn the terms of the debate, sidelining both Keynesianism and its socialist alternatives. In Britain and the United States the political interventions represented by Thatcherism and Reaganism established neo-liberalism as the new dominant common sense, the paradigm shaping all policies. In many ways this was its most important accomplishment. For a short period in the 1970s the view that there might be serious alternatives to capitalism was once again alive, but this was soon ended. Neo-liberalism provided new ways of justifying the basic institutions of the capitalist order, and it was rewarded with both economic and political success. A new phase of capitalist expansion began.

This political ascendancy of neo-liberal ideas could not be denied, but their rationality was still contested. One way of doing this became to contrast the relative influence of neo-liberalism in different models of capitalism. Neo-liberal ideas it was noticed had had greatest influence in the English-speaking world – the Anglosphere – and had less salience in other leading capitalist economies, particularly in countries in the European Union outside Britain, even in Germany where they had originated, or in East Asia, although they had been picked up and remorselessly applied in several countries outside the advanced economies, such as Chile. In these cases, neo-liberalism often took the form of technical economic advice, provided by teams of economists using ideas derived from mainstream neo-classical economics. After its military coup in 1973 Chile imported a team of economists from the University of Chicago to advise on the reshaping of its economy. This led to the suggestion that neo-liberal ideas were a defensive strategy to shore up a failing model of capitalism which was increasingly under pressure from more successful models, particularly Germany, Japan and Sweden. There was widespread incredulity at many of the policies which were prescribed by the Reagan Administration and the Thatcher Government and frequent predictions that while they might protect existing capitalist property in the short run, they would only do so by weakening the long-term performance of their national capitalisms, and endangering the stability and legitimacy of the liberal world order. The destruction of manufacturing capacity and the undermining of investment in both welfare and infrastructure were widely regarded as perverse, particularly when measured against the performance of other capitalist economies, which appeared to manage with much lower unemployment, higher growth and more generous welfare services. The idea that the United States and Britain in particular were being out-competed and left behind was very strong in the 1980s, at a time of vigorous debates about the causes of British and US decline. Neo-liberalism was still regarded as the ideology of an out-of-date capitalist model, which lacked the analytical tools to direct policy to appropriate remedies.

This view of neo-liberalism has remained influential and continued to inspire analyses in political economy of the policies that would be needed to reverse economic decline by making British and American capitalism more like German or East Asian capitalism. This perspective was weakened, however, by the resurgence of American and, to a lesser extent, British capitalism in the 1990s, and the difficulties encountered by other national capitalisms, particularly Germany, Japan and Sweden. By the end of the 1990s the triumphalism of US capitalism was back at full volume and neo-liberalism was unchallenged as the dominant ideology of the new world order proclaimed by the Americans and had become inseparable from the discourse of globalization. By this means the domestic and the global aspects of neo-liberalism tended to merge into a single doctrine, appropriate to the restored unity of the global economy.

The idea of national capitalisms accordingly began to give way to new analyses of capitalism as a global system of accumulation, allowing different assessments of the role of ideology and politics in capitalist societies. Many of the analyses of neo-liberalism as irrational were focused on national capitalisms and particular sectors, such as industrial capital. But treating capitalism as a global system of accumulation and looking at it from the standpoint of 'capital in general' rather than national or local capital, the rationality of neo-liberalism, and particularly its laissez-faire strand, as a political and economic strategy in the period of restructuring which occurred as a result of the 1970s stagflation is more apparent. Neo-liberalism gives priority to capital as money and therefore to the financial circuit of capital rather than to the production circuit. This means that the economy is viewed through the lens of finance rather than through the lens of industry, and so the priorities of finance come to predominate in the shaping of economic policy, and industry is expected to adjust to the rules that this establishes. In a period of rapid restructuring this has the advantage of enabling policies to be adopted which clear the decks, removing subsidies and protection, and freeing up capital from fixed positions. It allows capital to regain mobility, dissolving the spatial and institutional rigidities in which it had become encased. Neo-liberalism both promoted and legitimated the financial sector and its role in the economy. It did so by fiercely attacking the notion that industry created more real value than did finance and services, it helped develop new models of the financial sector and it promoted what became known as 'financialization'. This signified the attempt to reconstruct the finances of every organization and of every individual citizen to allow them to borrow and raise their spending. This tendency had long existed within modern financial economies, but now it was raised to a new height. Financialization became the driving force of the new growth model that was to power the 1990s boom.

From this perspective the contribution of neo-liberalism to the restructuring of capitalism was that it provided a means by which capital could begin to disengage from many of the positions and commitments which had been taken up during the Keynesian era at both the national and the international level. The ostensible priority of monetarism was to make sound money once more the cornerstone of economic policy, and to give up the Keynesian commitments to full employment and economic growth, and to planned development in the developing world. The issue was not whether monetarism as a technique could do what it claimed. In fact monetarism in its initial forms proved to be unworkable, because whichever indicator of money supply was used, governments found they then lost control of other forms of money. The real significance of monetarism was political. As Hayek noted, the key issue was to recognize that inflation was not a matter of technical error on the part of the monetary authorities, but of the political balance of power. Michal Kalecki's famous analysis in 1943 of the political significance of Keynesianism argued that it represented an alteration in the balance of power between labour and capital. If governments committed themselves to policies of full employment it meant a significant weakening of the normal capitalist disciplines of bankruptcy and unemployment and a substantial increase in the bargaining power of organized labour, particularly over wages. Neo-liberals argued that it was this which had led to the progressive extension of state intervention over the market economy in the form of wage and price controls, and the development of corporatist modes of governance.The political message of neo-liberalism was that the outcome of Keynesian political economy was accelerating inflation and growing state intervention. Making sound money once again the cornerstone of policy meant being prepared to take on politically all the vested interests which had grown up through the extended state and helped perpetuate the policies which were restricting the rights of managers to manage and were tying capital down in increasingly ossified economic and organizational structures.

Chief among these targets in the advanced capitalist economies were trade unions and the welfare state. As many costs as possible, it was argued, should be shifted from the state and back on to individuals, and markets, particularly labour markets, should be made as flexible as possible. Viewed from the standpoint of capital in general rather than of particular capitals, neo-liberalism offered a simple and straightforward criterion for the direction of policy. The presumption was always in favour of recreating the best conditions for markets to flourish, which meant removing as many restrictions on competition as possible, and empowering market agents by reducing the burdens of taxation. For such a policy to be effective the state had to be prepared to break the resistance of any group which demanded market protection or subsidy through the state. In practice there were many exceptions. Since the extended state of the last hundred years was built up precisely through the granting of such protections and subsidies to one group after another, such a task was fairly heroic in its ambitions. It implied unwinding not just the coils of social democracy but the coils of all forms of democracy, including those which were in the electoral interests of the right. The world's leading powers have always found it more agreeable to impose neo-liberal prescriptions on the 'failed states' of the periphery, rather than upon themselves.

As a result it has always been simpler to set out what a neo-liberal programme should be than actually to carry it through, particularly in the developed capitalist states. It has often been easier outside the advanced economies. The actual record of even the most neo-liberal regimes in the 1980s and 1990s were disappointing to many of their supporters, because they failed to make the dramatic inroads into state provision and taxation which were hoped for. Neo-liberal intellectuals were often as disillusioned with 'their' governments as socialist intellectuals have traditionally been with theirs.

One of the main reasons for this has been that neo-liberal governments in the capitalist core were beset by dilemmas. How far should they go in dismantling the state? How should they deal with corporate power? Could the state be reformed so that it merely polices the market order rather than intervening directly in the decisions which individuals should take? Could a liberal market order be reconciled with democracy and popular sovereignty? If it could not, how could the legitimacy of the market order be assured? Could the process of democracy be trusted to produce governments that uphold the rules constituting the market order? How could the principle of popular sovereignty be subordinated to the overriding requirement of safeguarding the principles of a market order without suspending democracy? If, however, a market order could only be sustained by an authoritarian government, how stable and permanent would such a regime be?

Neo-liberals, particularly those attracted to rational choice models of government, often assert that the pursuit of self-interest is the overriding factor in determining how individuals in both the public and private sectors behave. The difference is that in the private sector individuals are subject to competition, and the enforcement of these rules guarantees that choices are efficient and in the public interest. In the public sector there are no such checks, with the consequence that government departments and their budgets continually expand. The paradox for neo-liberals is that their revolution in government requires that a group of individuals be found who are not governed by self-interest, but motivated purely by the public good of upholding the rules of the market order. Yet if such a group existed it would contradict a basic premise of neo-liberal analysis. Since all power corrupts, even the most selfless neo-liberal government will soon find itself taking decisions which benefit the interests of the state or of corporate interests rather than the wider public.

One way out of this dilemma would be for neo-liberals to become libertarians and advocate the wholesale dismantling of the state, including state provision for defence and policing. But if one thing distinguishes neo-liberals it is that they believe in the importance of maintaining a minimal state and acknowledge that without certain of the functions which the state discharges the market order could not exist at all. This is the Hobbesian side of their dilemma. Should they agree to cede all power to the Sovereign and trust that the Sovereign will be benign and govern in accordance with neo-liberal principles? Their own analysis of human nature gives them no reason for thinking that the Sovereign will be anything but self-interested. The advent of democracy and the idea of popular sovereignty does not solve this problem. It intensifies it, since neo-liberals gloomily conclude that states gain even greater legitimacy by wrapping themselves in its mantle, and this emboldens them to interfere with the market in the name of the people, but in reality at the behest of all the special interests which come to infest the state and shape the policy of the government.

Granting the state absolute powers has, as a result, generally seemed too risky to liberals, so they move from the Hobbesian side of their dilemma to the Lockean, by trying to make the powers of the state as limited as possible. The traditional liberal device for doing this is to separate the powers of the state into executive, legislature and judiciary arms, and make the government directly accountable to the people through regular elections. But it has always been hard to make this balance of power work without paralysing the government or allowing one section to dominate, and it poses the dilemma starkly: can the people be trusted to protect the market order and make their electoral choices in line with true liberal principles? When the electorate was confined to those who owned substantial amounts of property, it was reasonable to suppose that they would have an interest in preserving the rules of the market order and could be relied on to ensure through the way they cast their votes that the government did the same. But once the notion of the people was widened to all citizens the difficulty of keeping the state minimal became acute, because it was obviously in the interests of politicians to promise benefits to particular groups of voters, spreading the costs over the whole body of citizens. This democratic ratchet, which saw each party in practice seeking to outbid every other party, gave the growth of the state an unstoppable momentum. This has presented neo-liberals with an unenviable choice – between trusting the sovereign or trusting the people. Both can threaten the market order.

In the eyes of neo-liberals the greatest failure of governments that have professed neo-liberal principles is that they have been unable to reverse the democratic ratchet and substantially reduce the size of the state. Despite all the rhetoric of rolling back the state, the actual accomplishments in the advanced economies were much more modest. Governments with strong neo-liberal programmes, such as the Thatcher Government in Britain, for example, generally ended up spending more when they left office than when they entered it. Neo-liberal governments have not been particularly successful at reducing the overall burden of taxation. Often it rose. What did change was the composition of public spending and of taxation. Spending on programmes such as housing and industry were often greatly reduced, but core welfare state programmes like education and health escaped. Spending on social security and welfare dependency continued to climb, but ways of financing this expenditure were shifted away from direct to indirect taxation. Such distributional changes often had important effects in building electoral coalitions behind neo-liberal programmes, but they did not amount to a substantial and permanent reduction in the size of the state. Neo-liberals around the world often dreamed of a government that would contemplate really radical free market experiments, such as abolishing inheritance and capital gains taxes altogether, introducing flat taxes, taking the axe to state education and state health programmes, obliging people instead to take out private insurance, stopping inflation protection for social security benefits, ending state support for higher education and introducing voucher schemes for schools. The nearest they came to it was the Labour Government in New Zealand in the 1980s, which launched probably the most ambitious neo-liberal programme attempted anywhere in the world, with massive cuts in subsidies, tariffs, spending and taxes, privatization of state assets, and the announcement of intentions to move towards a flat tax and minimum income scheme. When the experiment was halted by the dismissal of Roger Douglas, the Finance Minister, the Labour

Party split and some of the leading neo-liberals, including Roger Douglas and Derek Quigley, eventually established a new party, the Association of Consumers and Taxpayers. But it did not prosper.

The difficulty of engineering serious retrenchment in state spending caused neo-liberal governments to focus instead on how to make the public sector more efficient by introducing the disciplines of the market into the state. They embraced enthusiastically the techniques of the new public management, with its audits, targets, internal markets, performance indicators and emphasis upon outputs. But the new public management was not the same as privatization. It has certainly been used to involve the private sector much more in the delivery of public services, but its central thrust is not so much about shrinking the scale of government as expanding its scope. The new public management, with its mantras of enabling government, steering not rowing and the purchaser/provider split, was all about making the case for more active, efficient and effective government. But if government is more active, efficient and effective it is also likely to be more legitimate and to expand rather than to contract. Neo-liberals are caught again in a dilemma. If the state can be so reorganized that it delivers high quality public services, the need to privatize state services diminishes. On the whole, despite their rhetoric of rolling back the state, neo-liberal governments have devoted more time trying to get the public sector to perform better by importing managerial techniques from the private sector than to dismantle it. This commitment to technocratic managerialism was much more apparent than any faith in neo-liberal principles about trusting in markets to deliver. Markets were used as managerial tools in the pursuit of publicly determined objectives.

The broader difficulty for the laissez-faire strand of neo-liberalism is that capitalism needs democratic legitimacy if it is to survive, and welfare programmes ever since Bismarck and Chamberlain have been recognized in the leading capitalist governments as part of the price capital has to pay for that legitimacy. Dismantling welfare provision and trade unions might provide capital with some short-term benefits, but in the long run risks leading to a build-up of hostility and desperation among the poor and the propertyless. One of the arguments for welfare programmes which found support on both right and left was that such programmes were necessary to incorporate the mass of the population within the capitalist order and let everyone feel they had a stake in it. In the leading capitalist economies, democracy tended to be *social* democracy because mass electorates voted for parties which would deliver collective social provision, whether these were left of centre or right of centre. In the era of mass democracies, political parties of the right have always had to find programmes which could mobilize support, and often found it, like many European Christian Democratic parties, not in neo-liberal policies but in collectivist policies which promised security and protection. Laissez-faire seemed outmoded in the first half of the twentieth century, partly because it had such weak electoral appeal. A programme to preserve the general rules which allowed the market order to function and stripped away all the protections and benefits which had been secured over several generations was never likely to be wildly popular.

Neo-liberalism as an intellectual doctrine can be quite principled and inflexible, unwilling to contemplate compromises. But a number of politicians have been adroit at combining a neo-liberal economic programme with social conservative policies, and in recasting neo-liberal economic policies in ways that resonate as popular common sense. The authoritarian populism of Thatcher and Reagan were two such successful employments of neo-liberalism by politicians on the right. Both Thatcherism and Reaganism had their own special interests which were subsidized up to the hilt, but from this base they targeted particular vested interests and particular government programmes, although both presided over an expansion of government, in the case of Reagan a massive expansion because of the defence budget. But despite or perhaps because of these glaring inconsistencies they were also able to ram home their central ideological message that the age of big government was over, that governments existed to enable markets to work better, and to sustain the political and legal foundations of the market order. Thus were born these strange hybrids of conservative governments professing neo-liberal principles, and attempting to impose them on everyone except themselves.

The Washington Consensus

In the 1990s the revival of the United States economy appeared to reinforce the neo-liberal message. By this time neo-liberalism had became associated with the new discourse about globalization. One version of the policy implications of this new world order was the 'Washington Consensus', a phrase coined by John Williamson to describe the policies which the international institutions based in Washington, the International Monetary Fund (IMF), the World Bank and the US Treasury Department, had come to favour for countries in Latin America and other parts of the world which were seeking to develop their economies and receive support from the international community. The short version of the Washington Consensus was 'stabilize, privatize and liberalize'; the longer version enjoined fiscal discipline, tax reform, competitive exchange rates, liberalization of trade and foreign direct investment, privatization of state enterprises, deregulation, investment in human capital and infrastructure, and enforcement of property rights.

Critics of the Washington Consensus saw it as seeking to impose a neo-liberal model as the template for the whole world, which ignored the very different needs of particular economies, in particular the need for developing economies to protect their industries while they were getting established. This was the policy which all the leading economic powers had followed in the past, but which they now sought to deny to developing economies, insisting instead that to have access to the markets of the rich countries they must agree to liberalize their own markets first. But developing economies had little choice, and many of them attempted to apply the neo-liberal disciplines in their domestic policies by this means, hoping to integrate into the global economy. Only a few states, like China, were able to bargain effectively and limit their exposure to competition by, for example, holding down their exchange rate.

At the height of the neo-liberal era, after the fall of the Soviet Union, neo-liberalism seemed all-conquering, and its ascendancy for a time was unquestioned. The challenges that did come were from within neo-liberalism itself. The laissez-faire and social market strands of neo-liberalism in particular became sharply delineated in the debates around the global economy and the appropriate institutions for it. There was a vigorous debate over models of capitalism and later varieties of capitalism, in which a distinction was drawn between liberal market economies and coordinated market economies. Liberal market economies were found predominantly in the Anglosphere, and were noted for their commitment to privatization, deregulation and liberalization, flexible labour markets, shareholder value, residual welfare states and the acceptance of the dominance of financial markets. Coordinated market economies included the original six members of the European Union, the Scandinavian countries and several of the East Asian countries. Here there was still commitment to long-term industrial investment, the interests of all stakeholders, a comprehensive welfare state, restrictions on liberalization and a reduced role for the financial markets.

The laissez-faire strand of neo-liberalism believed that what was needed was for states to get out of the way of the global market, and allow the benign processes of competition to work their magic. Privatization, deregulation, open borders, free trade, low tax regimes were the engines of progress. National governments and their protectionist policies and interventionist bureaucracies were the main obstacles to global prosperity. This analysis extended among some of the more radical neo-liberals to many of the existing institutions of the global economy, including the World Bank and the IMF, which were regarded, along with the United Nations and the whole programme of foreign aid, as misguided political intervention in the global economy. Foreign aid was treated as a welfare programme at the international level which should be scrapped. The World Bank and the IMF were considered to be embryonic forms of a global government and were criticized for thinking of the global economy in Keynesian terms.

Those neo-liberals who saw the merits of coordinated market economies, at least in some sectors, also tended to recognize that the stability of the global economy did require a certain level of institutionalization, the formation in effect of a minimal state for the global level, paralleling some of the functions which the state performed at the national level. In this way a new role for organizations like the IMF, the World Bank and the World Trade Organization (WTO) was devised. They were to become the agents for fostering the kind of policies and institutions, both national and international, which would make it easier for countries to enter the global market. Programmes for structural adjustment, investment in human capital, good governance and the building of social capital all followed. From a social market perspective, interventions to reform the WTO and end the protectionist policies of the US and the EU, to advance the Kyoto agreements on climate change and even tentative steps to address questions of the vast disparities in wealth and resources between different parts of the global economy could all be justified.

Prospects for Neo-liberalism

Some of the most perceptive observers of the international political economy in the 1990s doubted that neo-liberalism would last. Robert Cox, drawing on Karl Polanyi, argued that neo-liberalism as a political and ideological project should be understood as the successor to the economic liberalism of the nineteenth century, the ideological and political project which had been responsible for the free market experiments of that time. Resistance to the consequences of free market policies from right and left had led to the extension of collective control and regulation of the market in the twentieth century. The adoption of neo-liberalism both reflected and helped accelerate the breakdown of those systems of control and regulation and the unleashing once more of the free market. Cox suggested that the effect of the application of neo-liberal policies throughout the world would produce eventually a strong political reaction and the re-regulation of capital at some point in the future, and the preservation of a strong global economy. The consequence of failure would be the fracturing of the global economy into antagonistic and protectionist regional blocs.

A different assessment of neo-liberalism gave less weight to it as a global ideology, and instead emphasized how competitive pressures force the convergence of all capitalist models and all national economies on neo-liberal institutions and policies, such as privatization, deregulation, shareholder value, flexible labour markets and residual welfare. There was debate over just how strong these pressures for convergence are, and whether they could be resisted. The debate looks a little curious in the wake of the financial crash. No-one will be asking for a while whether states can resist the pressures towards neo-liberal policies. They are all too resistible just now. But that does not mean they may not revive in the future. Three decades of neo-liberalism have left their mark, and in important respects there is no going back. The financialization of the economy will be very hard to reverse, because it is not just a question of the use of private finance in the public sector, but the penetration of financialization deep into everyday life and consciousness. Many citizens have become so used to credit, debt and financial calculation, savings and investment, the mortgage culture, that even such a shock as the present downturn is unlikely to change their behaviour for very long. When they are given the opportunity they will want to resume where they have been forced to leave off.

The ascendancy of neo-liberalism in the 1990s was captured in the idea of disciplinary neo-liberalism – the imposition of neo-liberal policies on all countries seeking to participate in the global economy. The agents of this discipline were the international agencies such as the IMF and the World Bank, through the conditions they attached to their loans, but also the financial markets themselves, with their constant threat to mark down a currency or the credit rating of a government if policies were pursued which were outside those prescribed by neo-liberalism. The sanctions of the institutions were direct and highly political, but the sanctions of the markets were impersonal, willed by no one single person, but created by the decisions of many thousands of investors and companies. A variant of this idea, known as depoliticization, was the observed trend under neo-liberalism for more and more decisions to be transferred from the control of elected politicians in national governments and handed to unelected agencies. Making central banks independent became one of the best known of these, but it spread into many different spheres. Handing power to unelected experts might seem contrary to neo-liberal principles, but, provided the experts were prepared to take decisions in the light of neo-liberal precepts, it was acceptable. In this way the quango state, which expanded enormously in the neo-liberal era, became an important instrument through which many neo-liberal policies were delivered.

Neo-liberalism has appeared in many different forms since it first emerged, hydra-headed, in the 1970s. No sooner did its opponents cut off one head than another has appeared, hissing all the louder. What has to be avoided, however, is a tendency to treat neo-liberalism as a phenomenon which manifests itself everywhere and in everything. It is better to analyze neo-liberalism by breaking it up into the different doctrines and ideas which compose it, and then exploring how they are related to particular practices and political projects, rather than treating 'neo-liberalism' as though it is the source of everything, from Angela Merkel to global poverty. European social democracy, for example, has plainly been influenced by neo-liberal ideas, but to suggest that it has become simply an expression of neo-liberalism is too simple a judgement. Many other factors are at work. Ideologies are extremely important, but ideological determinism is in the end no better than economic determinism, and no more illuminating. The history of neo-liberalism shows that, like other ideologies, there is no pure form of it, and no single authoritative statement, and within its compass there can be found both highly subtle and extraordinarily crude versions. There are also a number of different political forms which it can take, a variety of hybrids and compounds. Much energy has been profitably spent identifying the links between neo-liberals and conservatives, including neo-conservatives, as well as social democrats.

All that may now change. It used to be asked whether within the confines of capitalist global economy there is any alternative to neo-liberalism, and some argued that so total had become the domination of capital and so one-dimensional the discourses surrounding it that the only possible opposition was total opposition from outside the system altogether. Such a view will not have been altered by the financial crash. It is profoundly pessimistic because it implies that only total overthrow of existing power relations from below or from without offers any prospect of change. Neo-liberalism itself, however, has offered many examples of how in practice attempts to implement neo-liberal programmes both in developed and developing countries have highlighted inconsistencies in its ordering principles, producing conflicts and creating different sets of political possibilities. The great implosion of neo-liberal confidence and belief in the 2008 crash also creates new opportunities for re-evaluating its record, and opening political debates on what should be preserved and what discarded.

By 2008, in a sense which was true but rather unenlightening, all governments throughout the global economy were neo-liberal governments, because they were obliged to operate within a set of common structures in the global economy which reflected, however imperfectly, neo-liberal principles. Neo-liberalism, like globalization, was not monolithic or proceeding in a single direction. It was also vulnerable. It encouraged irrational exuberance, it helped inflate the bubbles, and eventually they burst. Sometimes it was neo-liberal financiers and central bankers who burst them. Neo-liberalism needs understanding in all its different aspects and in its many contradictions, which create different political spaces and possible outcomes. The two faces of neo-liberalism, on the one hand, the iconoclastic, ground-clearing, radical impulse to tear down the obstacles to capital accumulation and, on the other, the concern for using the state to ensure the democratic legitimacy of the market order and to create the kind of institutions which encourage participation and limit the destructive impacts of free markets, are often in conflict and will continue to determine the way in which this doctrine develops.

Richard Robison has argued that markets need empires, in the sense that the market order by itself is a fragile thing, and needs the protection of non-market institutions and a range of public goods which only the state can provide. But empires if they are to be stable need to become hegemonic – they have to be inclusive, not simply dominant. The great strength of laissez-faire neo-liberalism is its understanding of the logic of capitalism, and the needs of the corporations that now drive the process of accumulation. Its great weakness is its blindness to the consequences of failing to attend to the effects of the global economy it helped create on global poverty, on the environment, on the legitimacy of the global political order and on the stability of the financial order. Before the crash of 2008 neo-liberalism, as a doctrine and as a project, had already mutated. After the crash it will struggle to survive in its previous form, and will probably mutate some more. But although it may suffer an eclipse for a while, the reasons why it rose to prominence in the first place have not gone away.

Neo-liberalism and globalization have been the two ascendant discourses for thirty years, and both helped legitimate and engineer the successful reordering of capitalism both politically and economically after the 1970s crisis. Neo-liberalism in its different forms was especially valuable in helping to articulate the new financial growth model, identifying what was wrong with Keynesianism and the extended state, and finding a new policy direction in the form of privatization, liberalization and deregulation. Much of the deregulation that occurred in the neo-liberal era, as Michael Moran has pointed out, also involved re-regulation, the establishment of different kinds of agencies and regulatory bodies overseeing a freer market. This was for the most part light-touch regulation and the aim of policy was to remove obstacles to the fullest possible development of the global economy, and the financial institutions played an increasingly dominant role in this. In the Anglosphere countries in particular some of the institutions and practices which had developed since the 1930s were stripped out in these years, which made the Anglo-Saxon model of capitalism, the liberal market economy, more distinct than ever. The Anglosphere economies flourished in the 1990s boom, and achieved some extraordinary results. Ireland emerged as the Celtic tiger, with very rapid growth rates, fuelled by a huge inward investment boom, and a very favourable tax and regulatory regime for foreign businesses. The UK economy grew continuously between 1993 and 2008, the longest boom in its modern history, and in marked contrast to its post-war cycles of stop-go and boom and bust.

Central to this recovery was the United States economy and its ability to reorganize the global economy in ways which allowed the conditions for a new boom to be established, while maintaining US dominance. The term 'Washington Consensus' was quickly accepted because it seemed to sum up the experience of many countries in their dealing with the rich countries in the neo-liberal era, that they were forced to fall in line with a number of policy priorities which were formulated in the international agencies dominated by the United States. The boom of the 1990s seemed to vindicate neo-liberalism and the growth model it had devised. It allowed a new period of sustained general expansion in the global economy under American leadership, which had not seemed at all likely in the 1980s, when much of the talk was of US decline. The expansion came at a price, however, and as in previous booms the flaws and cracks in the growth model were covered over or ignored. Too many of those who were participating in the boom suspended judgement and somehow convinced themselves, even as they read Charles Kindleberger on *Manias, Panics, and Crashes*, that those things happened a long time ago, and this time things would be different. They were different, but not in the way that neo-liberals had hoped.

4

The Politics of Recession

As the credit crunch of 2007 turned into the financial crash of 2008, increasing concerns were voiced that worse was to follow, and that the crash would turn into a global recession, which if it proved deep and long enough could produce a more generalized crisis of the whole economic and political system. The IMF World Economic Outlook published in January 2009 and discussed in Chapter 2 predicted that for the first time since 1945 the advanced economies taken as a whole would experience a contraction of economic activity in 2009. By 2010, however, it was expecting a modest recovery, and for the rising economies, it predicted a slowdown in economic growth in 2009, but then a sharp increase in 2010.

All predictions in this crisis are, however, surrounded by huge uncertainties. The IMF is an authoritative source, but its predictions in January 2009 were substantially different from the predictions in its previous economic outlook published six months before. Most of its forecasts were substantially marked down, because of the speed of deterioration in the global economy. Such reports can only be compiled on the basis of the evidence that is available at the time, and fast-moving global financial events can create new realities which were not imagined a few months earlier. The next World Economic Outlook will almost certainly change the predictions again, and few expect it to be in a positive direction. At some point the bottom in the market will be reached, but when and where no-one can be sure.

All that can be said with confidence is that, like all past global recessions, this recession will vary across different national economies and regions; some countries will be much more severely hit than others, some will be relatively insulated – Canada is a good example – but very few will be completely immune. If the recession turns out to be short and shallow, and growth is quickly resumed, then the crisis will be downgraded, and all the melodrama and the gloom during 2008 will look hugely exaggerated, a media and political storm with few lasting effects. A brief crisis would mean too that not much would really need to change either in politics or in economics. It could be back to business as usual, with minimum disruption. This kind of recession has a V shape; a sharp downturn and a sharp recovery. It is the shape predicted in the charts of the IMF, which sees a swift bounce back of the global economy in 2010 after the contraction in 2009.

Things will be very different if the recession turns out to be shaped like an L. This pushes the economy into depression territory, where economic growth is substantially below trend for several years, and at times more than 20 per cent below. This is the kind of recession which the United States suffered in the 1930s. The downturn was extremely sharp, if not quite vertical in 1930 and 1931, but instead of the recovery being immediate and decisive, economic activity became very flat and, although the trough was reached in 1932, and a recovery did begin in 1933, it was fragile, and there was a further setback in 1937. Overall the economy remained in a depressed condition with a high margin of unused capacity, until the switch to rearmament and conscription in the Second World War. In that respect the Great Depression was shaped more like a W than an L. What made it a depression was not that there was no growth, but that the growth was not sustained to the point where it became a new boom, recovering all the ground that had previously been lost. Something similar happened to the Japanese economy after 1990. Once the economy had fallen into a deflationary hole, it proved very hard for the government to rescue it, and rebuild the confidence and trust that a growing economy needs. A deflationary recession if it once takes hold can last a long time, a decade of no growth or below-average growth. Economies plunged into depression make governing much more difficult, because there is so little for governments to give away, and constant sacrifices have to be demanded from citizens. There is no growth dividend and politics becomes focused on the redistribution of existing burdens and the sharing out of new ones. This is why governments will do everything they can to avoid deflation.

In the 1970s the problem was not deflation but inflation, how to master inflationary expectations and deal with the various price shocks which had produced the vicious combination of high and accelerating inflation with stagnant and falling production, employment and profitability. But in one sense the politics of inflation and deflation are similar, because in both it is the steep changes in prices, whether up or down, which creates the uncertainty and increasingly extreme political responses. The key political issue which always arises is how the burdens of adjustment which the inflation or deflation is forcing on the economy are to be shared. If the government does nothing, then the market will distribute the losses and gains in an

effective but almost certainly deeply illegitimate and politically unacceptable manner, outraging many different elements within the democracy,
triggering large-scale protests and widespread disaffection.

Doing nothing was the policy preference of President Hoover who,
unfortunately for him, was elected President in 1928 and took office just
before the Great Crash. His response to the Great Crash and the slide into
depression was mercilessly lampooned much later by J.K. Galbraith. But
in the context of the time and the prevailing conventional wisdom, his
behaviour could not be faulted. Direct intervention by government, it was
believed, would worsen the problems rather than improve them. The only
safe course for government in a recession was to put its own house in order,
balance the budget, batten down the hatches and see out the storm. The
markets had always corrected themselves in the past and laid the foundations for recovery. There was nothing government could do directly to aid
this natural healing process.

This attitude had dominated classical liberalism for a century. It was the
attitude on display during the Irish famine between 1845 and 1849 in
which up to one million died and another million were forced to emigrate
out of a population of eight million. The death toll was not caused but was
certainly not helped by the British Government's refusal to stop the profitable export of corn from Ireland, which could have been distributed to
those who were starving. Many believed that governments should not
intervene or attempt to play God where markets were concerned. At a
certain point in the development of democracy this position became unsustainable. Governments could not be indifferent to the suffering of their citizens, and could not afford to be seen to be idle. The inaction of the British
and American governments at the start of the Great Depression provided a
marker against which all future governments were judged. All governments, even the most reactionary, were obliged to become activist, or at
least promise action during downturns.

Neo-liberalism and the Return of the State

Neo-liberalism did not really depart from this. Its adoption as the ruling
common sense in the 1980s and 1990s did not mark a return to classical
liberalism, or to some of the extreme laissez-faire attitudes current in the
nineteenth century. It continued the tradition of active government which
Keynesianism had helped legitimate. It did not dispute the idea that

government was ultimately responsible for what happened in the economy. In political economy terms the insight of Keynesianism was a very simple one – the size of government in the modern economy and the expectations of modern citizens made it impossible for government to stand aside and treat recessions as though they were natural events outside government control. In practice they still might be, and governments might have few levers to control them, but this became a position very hard to advance politically. In the current recession few have attempted to rehearse this argument. They prefer the argument that the crisis is the fault of governments and the regulators. But that suggests that in principle a better form of regulation exists which could avoid these mistakes.

This attempt to blame government has not saved neo-liberalism from some hard knocks. The consequences of the crisis for neo-liberalism as the ruling discourse in political economy during the last thirty years are discussed in Chapter 3, but it is already clear that it has suffered some damage from its association with the financial growth model of recent times. Some of the high priests of neo-liberalism, such as Alan Greenspan, a former associate of Ayn Rand, who always radiated extreme confidence in the ability of markets to create stability and cautioned against increasing regulation, have come in for severe criticism. He retired just before the crash, but he is blamed for not anticipating it, and if he did anticipate it for doing nothing to forestall it.

A certain strand of neo-liberalism already looks therefore like one of the main ideological casualties of the recession, in the same way that a certain kind of social democracy was a casualty in the 1970s. Neo-liberalism had espoused an anti-state rhetoric, and many of its specific policy measures had been aimed at reducing the involvement of the state in many policy areas, through the encouragements of deregulation of private business and privatization of state assets. But although neo-liberals encouraged the dismantling of many of the institutional arrangements and outward forms of the post-war state, they did not reduce very much the scope or scale of the state. They merely redirected its energy and its targets. The state remained very intrusive in the lives of its citizens, particularly through the continual programme of reform and reorganization launched in public sectors around the world.

One of the forms of neo-liberal governance, 'depoliticization', was discussed in Chapter 3. It is the attempt by governments in several countries to divest themselves of responsibility for particular policy areas by delegating that responsibility to arms-length agencies. It involved the attempt to take the politics out of decision-making, and instead of allowing politicians and legislatures to be involved in the decisions, to hand them over to boards of experts, who were unelected and only indirectly accountable for their decisions. The most high-profile instance of depoliticization was the increasing trend, encouraged by the IMF, for governments to give up any direct control over monetary policy, and instead hand it to an independent central bank. One of the central criticisms which monetarists had made of Keynesianism was that the attempt to fine tune demand through fiscal means produced a political business cycle rather different from the old capitalist business cycle. Politicians had huge temptations and opportunities to attempt to influence the economic climate just before elections, and then to clamp down and reverse policy once elected. Bribing voters with their own money was the charge; its effectiveness was disputed, and the empirical evidence was always weak, but the idea took hold, particularly in the financial markets, that governments in a democracy could not be trusted to behave responsibly and would always intervene in the economy to boost the feel-good factor just before elections. Over several election cycles the result was to impart a strong inflationary bias to the economy.

Making central banks independent, or at least giving them defined responsibilities for managing monetary policy and interest rates, and taking these matters out of the hands of treasuries and finance departments appeared to be a throwback to the days of the gold standard when central bankers jealously guarded the integrity of the monetary system, and strove to find ways to make it 'politician proof'. The gold standard worked best, it was argued by champions of the gold standard like Montagu Norman, the Governor of the Bank of England from 1920 to 1944, if its operation was regarded as akin to a natural process which no-one could tamper with, least of all governments. In this way its consequences were viewed as automatic and inevitable, and could not be altered. All market agents and governments needed to work within them, even if some of the consequences, such as the acceptance of deflation for debtor countries, were unpalatable. If all major countries accepted the gold standard rules then the benefit, it was suggested, was a massive boost to confidence and the reduction of uncertainty. By being linked to gold, sterling as the main reserve currency was rock solid and could be treated for all practical purposes as being as good as gold.

The 2008 crisis exposed the limits of depoliticization, just as the 1929 crisis exposed the limits of the gold standard. The severity of the crisis swept away the orthodoxy and compelled governments to become directly involved. Thirty years of rhetoric about the incompetence of politicians and bureaucrats, how markets were always smarter than governments and how governments should always seek to do less rather than more and learn to trust the superior wisdom of the markets, melted away like summer dew once the fierce heat of the crisis was felt. The return of the state was demanded by commentators, bankers and politicians who not long before had been celebrating the infallibility of finance and worshipping at the shrine of efficient markets. They did not seem so efficient in September 2008 when the whole financial edifice of western capitalism briefly wobbled, and the risk of catastrophe was only narrowly averted. It was averted by recourse to that most old-fashioned of remedies, the collective power of the community represented in the sovereign power of the state. For all the vaunted independence of the market, its ultimate dependence on the state, which political economists had never doubted, was once again laid bare. In a crisis only the state has the resources and capacity to intervene to save the market from itself.

Only the state has the ability also to reorganize capitalism and create the conditions for a new period of expansion. That does not always mean the state will succeed. It merely underlines the fact that, however much under capitalism it may appear that economics drives politics, the market cannot dispense with politics, however much market agents and market ideologists might like to pretend that the market does not need the state. In a crisis many of these same market ideologists become pragmatists and recognize the necessity for swift and decisive state intervention. This should come as no surprise. In their diagnosis of the 1970s stagflation, and of the failings of the overextended state both of Lyndon Johnson's Great Society programme in the United States and of European social democracy, neo-liberals always saw the need for decisive political action to break the power of key special interests such as the trade unions, to reform the state and to set new and much more flexible rules for the operation of markets. None of this would have happened without political will and political struggle, and neo-liberals were very much aware of it. But the battle won, some neo-liberals became complacent, supposing that the market nirvana had arrived and that nothing fundamental could now go wrong. Governments could take their cues from the markets, and just play an enabling role, so that markets could reach their full potential. As Peter Gowan has argued, bubbles could even be manipulated by the leading banks with the tacit approval of the financial authorities to restructure world markets in ways that favoured their interests. Blowing bubbles up and then bursting them without destabilizing the entire global financial system became a special skill. This partly explains why governments often seemed to treat the bubbles that the 1990s expansion was creating with indifference, as well as the warning signs from elsewhere in the global economy – the Asian financial crisis in 1997 and the dot.com bubble in 2000. The markets themselves would take care of it. The financial heartlands of western capitalism in New York, London and Frankfurt were thought to be immune from the problems experienced elsewhere. This was a spectacular misjudgement, and the fact that so many governments of different political colours, so many banks and financial institutions, so many commentators and pundits were implicated in it only made the crash when it came so much more devastating for their credibility, and for the credibility of the neo-liberal order which up to then had seemed so solid.

The politics of recession often leads to the questioning of current orthodoxies and a ruthless reassessment of former beliefs and assumptions. The discrediting of a dominant set of assumptions creates new opportunities and new narratives. They do not always win through. The old order does not give up without a fight, since powerful interests have become associated with it and they resist change, and maintain that there is no reason why things should not go on in the old way. But new interests, as well as those interests subordinated within the old regime and forced to accommodate to it, now seize the initiative to press their case. If the crisis is deep enough and prolonged enough then the result can be a period of turbulence in ideology and in politics, in which a range of outcomes becomes possible. The old order can reassert itself, although often in a different form; there can be a prolonged period of confusion; there can be separate national solutions, and the breakdown of any sense of an overarching world order; or there can be the gradual emergence of a new world order and a new political and ideological dispensation. This happened eventually as a result of the Great Depression; it happened as a result of the stagflation in the 1970s. Might it happen again? Certainly many of the ingredients are in place, but some are distinctly lacking. The forces arrayed against the neo-liberal order look comparatively weak, and there is as yet no compelling alternative vision of how the global economy might be ordered, what the steps towards it might be, and what an alternative political economy to neo-liberalism might look like. The debates around these issues will be explored further in the last two chapters.

Who Gains? Who Loses?

Distributional questions always come to the fore in recessions. Once an economy is shrinking, the question of how the reduced income is to be shared out becomes critical. Much of the redistribution is achieved through the mechanism of price changes, whether upwards or downwards. Any rapid price changes favour those who are able to switch out of fixed positions and reorganize their assets. That is why it is always those on fixed incomes or with limited assets or the ability to make their assets liquid who suffer in an inflation or in a deflation. But because the income and prospects of so many people are affected, and often affected seriously, the potential for major pressure on the government, in some countries leading to riots and serious civil unrest, is always present.

In a recession stories that always feature prominently in the media are the tales of individuals suddenly brought low, whether by miscalculation or by fraud. Stories like that of Bernard Madoff, the US financier who faced allegations in 2008 that he had defrauded investors in his company of $50 billion, have a peculiar fascination. It is not the sheer size of the sums involved, or the fact that it is particularly novel. There were numerous financial scandals during the bubble years, including those concerning Enron and Robert Maxwell. What makes Madoff special is that he was at the heart of the New York financial community, a former chairman and founder of NASDAQ, a key stock market index, and someone who was admired and trusted. Madoff lived the part he was expected to play. His website coolly announced his personal credo to the world:

> In an era of faceless organisations owned by other equally faceless organisations, Bernard L. Madoff Investment Securities LLC harks back to an earlier era in the financial world. The owner's name is on the door. Clients know that Bernard Madoff has a personal interest in maintaining the unblemished record of value, fair-dealing and high ethical standards that has always been the firm's hallmark.

Madoff seems to have operated a classic Ponzi scheme, named after Charles Ponzi who achieved notoriety for a fraud in Boston in 1920. Ponzi set up an investment company and advertised very high returns to investors, attracting large numbers of depositors all eager to become rich. But the deposits, instead of being invested, were used directly to pay the returns promised to previous investors. The actual income from investments never matched the money that had to be paid out. Such a scheme, to be viable, therefore needed to attract ever higher levels of deposits to pay the high returns that the scheme guaranteed and which were the source of its attractiveness. When the police finally raided Ponzi's offices they discovered that he had assets worth only $61 (he had received $7.9 million from investors). Madoff offered high premium rates to investors, but how he was able to do so never seems to have been properly explored by those who took up his offer. Apparently his high standing and reputation were enough. People had to be recommended by other rich investors to get into his scheme. Applicants were informed by those in the know that it was difficult to be accepted, which made people all the more eager to try, and all the more pleased when they were. Everyone assumed that the high returns, which never seemed to vary, must be due to his outstanding financial acumen, and that he had found a way like the alchemists of old to turn base metal into gold. But he had not. Those who did ask questions were politely blocked and told to invest somewhere else. The regulators did not question the rather peculiar arrangements for the audit of the company. Leading members of the financial community in New York and around the world were duped, along with many thousands of investors who entrusted their money to him, or money that had been entrusted to them to invest. One French financial investor killed himself after learning that the millions his clients had entrusted to him and which he had handed over to Madoff had vanished.

The financial markets have always spawned scandals. What was remarkable about the Madoff scandal was that this alleged fraud was not set up by a plausible small-time swindler like Ponzi and perpetrated on gullible financially unsophisticated personal investors. It originated within the heart of the financial community, by one of its best-known names, and it apparently deceived many of the most sophisticated players and analysts, as well as the regulators. It is an illustration of how, during bubbles, ordinary judgement can be suspended. So long as there is human credulity there will always be those who seek to take advantage of it. Scandals like this demonstrate that no-one potentially is immune.

Following the outcome of Madoff's trial, his name is now likely to be forever linked with the 2008 crash. The disappearance of the funds which were entrusted to him is not in doubt. He will become a symbol for what was wrong with Wall Street and the whole culture of financial capitalism which neo-liberals encouraged in the 1980s and took decisive steps to create. As he put it on his website, the problem with the present era of capitalism is that citizens have to deal with faceless organizations. It is hard to hold corporate leaders and financiers to account when things go wrong because no-one knows who they are and they mostly refuse to appear on the media to defend themselves. But in Madoff's case his arrest made him the scapegoat, the face of the financial collapse.

The search for people to blame will intensify in the years ahead. The same process was visible in the 1930s. One of the most high-profile scapegoats who came to stand for everything the public hated about Wall Street was Richard Whitney, the President of the New York Stock Exchange, who spent most of the early years of the Depression assuring investors that there was no reason to be alarmed and that recovery would happen soon. Later in that decade he was indicted and eventually jailed on fraud charges, and his trial became symbolically the trial of Wall Street itself. Wall Street eventually recovered, making the careers of Bernard Madoff and many others possible, but it took a long time. Restrictive regulation was imposed on the financial sector in a bid to make finance responsible and accountable, and to tie it down, separating investment from retail banking so that in future lending would be cautious and prudent, and speculative frenzies would be avoided. This mood of making finance the servant of enterprise rather than the master lasted through the first part of the long post-war boom, but by the 1970s these restrictions were perceived as some of the obstacles that were holding back economic advance. The discrediting of the Keynesian and social democratic regimes allowed the new philosophy of deregulation and arms-length regulation to flourish. The more successful the new financial economy appeared, the more political pressure developed to take the shackles off, and this was accomplished by the 1990s in a number of countries, particularly Britain and the United States and other countries in the Anglosphere. The financial sector became the driver for the new financial growth model. The countries that were to form the eurozone were more resistant, but not completely.

The Political Fallout

Major fraudsters are an easy target, but also a misleading one. A very small number of financiers actually act illegally. A few may be found to have defrauded their investors in an illegal manner, but many millions of investors have lost money in schemes which were entirely legal, and above suspicion, as a general consequence of the decline of market values. The

Queen of England lost £25 million, and quite reasonably enquired, when she visited the London School of Economics in November 2008, that, as she put it, 'If these things were so large how come everybody missed them?' The banking collapse meant huge losses in savings accounts, pensions, housing, with further consequences for employment. In the politics of recession, one of the first questions becomes, 'Who is to blame for creating this mess?' Governments are an easy target for public anger, on the assumption that if something bad has happened, the government has failed to prevent it from happening and is therefore culpable. That makes recessions usually a hard time for incumbent governments. Many governments will become victims of the recession, voted out of office because their response is judged too feeble or too incompetent by their voters, and if the crisis is great enough it is almost impossible for governments not to appear feeble and incompetent. Governments can never act quickly enough to satisfy their voters. The safety valve which Schumpeter argued that democracy offers to capitalism is a regular alternation of leaders, and immediate pressures can sometimes be relieved by changing the party in government. No incumbent government will be safe during this crisis and many will fall.

Authoritarian regimes sometimes perish altogether because they do not have such flexibility. Even in democracies popular unrest and riots can force a change of leaders. One of the first casualties of the recession was the government of Iceland in January 2009, when riots precipitated ministerial resignations and the calling of early elections, and the resignation of the Prime Minister, Geir Haarde. Iceland had prospered in the previous two decades by encouraging a large financial sector, one of the largest in proportion to the size of its economy in the world. The people of Iceland had enjoyed one of the world's highest standards of living, partly as a result of this. Iceland's banks were major players in global financial markets, and its leading bankers had stakes in many companies in Europe and the United States, even owning football clubs. The sub-prime crisis meant huge losses for the Iceland banks, and they had to be rescued by the Iceland Government. The banking collapse was followed by the collapse of the currency, since foreign investors were no longer prepared to lend to the Icelandic Government. The economy went into a nosedive, and interest rates and inflation both soared to around 18 per cent. Savers suffered huge losses. As a small country, Iceland was suddenly exposed and vulnerable and a strong lobby emerged for immediate entry to the European Union, and even to the euro, if it could be secured, in order to give Iceland some protection. The bitterness of the Icelandic people at the sudden collapse of their prosperity and their future prospects was vented on the government, and it was almost instantly forced out. One demonstrator said: 'We had a good country and they ruined it.'

The same process can be seen at work throughout the democratic world. There have been riots and strikes in a growing number of countries, including France, Latvia, Greece and Britain. Incumbent governments are increasingly unpopular. There was a particularly dramatic effect on the United States presidential race. Barack Obama's victory became certain and substantial once the scale of the financial crash and the likely consequences for the rest of the economy became clear in September 2008. Although the Democrats had considerable responsibility both during the Clinton presidency and in Congress during the Bush years for the policies that had stoked the boom and relaxed regulation of the markets, the bulk of the American electorate appeared to blame the Bush administration more, and John McCain, the Republican nominee, was perceived as too close to George Bush despite his attempts to distance himself. Obama was able to use his rhetoric of change to suggest that he was best placed to cope with the economic downturn and to sort out the economic mess the next president would inherit. His policy programme contained relatively few specifics; the rhetoric of change was sufficient.

Part of the reason why the financial crisis was so destructive for the Republicans in the US was that the party, ever since Reagan, had been strongly linked with the neo-liberal programme. They had been the champions of supply-side economics and financial deregulation. They had promoted the virtues of the American model as superior to the capitalist models of Germany and Japan, and there had been much premature bragging when the US was riding so spectacularly high at the end of the 1990s, while Japan was still to emerge from its ten-year stagnation, Europe's growth was still sluggish, and its unemployment relatively high. But the fruits of this great boom had not been evenly spread, and most American wages had stagnated or only increased slightly since the 1980s. The big beneficiaries of the financial boom were the American rich, who multiplied in number and increased their share of total national wealth. With the souring of the boom, coming on top of two unpopular wars, there was a significant shift of opinion away from the Republicans. Obama was the beneficiary, but any Democratic candidate in 2008 would have done well.

The election of Obama is potentially a watershed in US politics, since he has the rare opportunity to shape a new coalition and make some fundamental changes to US domestic and foreign policy. He is not short of vision on what he wants to do, but it is as yet unclear whether he can build the capacities both political and organizational that will be necessary to get the changes that he wants. The New Deal programme which Franklin Roosevelt cautiously improvised and experimented with in his first three terms caused bitter divisions in American politics, and was only partially successful in overcoming the Depression. Its legacy and its achievements are still contested, but it set the framework of American politics for the next four decades. Roosevelt was fortunate because he was able to concentrate on a programme of domestic recovery, and won re-election in 1936 and 1940 on the strength of it, even though his policies had not ended the Depression. In part this was because there was no revival of the international economy. After the gold standard had broken down and apart from some desultory international conferences there was no realistic prospect of restoring a unified liberal world order. The US chose to put all its energies into attempting to rebuild its domestic economy and largely ignored both international politics and international economics for a decade. The US was such a large and relatively self-contained economy that this was a feasible strategy at that time.

Obama is not so fortunate. He inherits not just a stricken domestic economy but also a stricken global economy, and a global economy which has been shaped and reshaped by the United States since 1945, and which the United States still takes the lead in governing. Reconciling the demands of global leadership with domestic popularity will be far from easy, and Obama has fewer resources to deal with this than previous post-war presidents. Jimmy Carter in 1976 won the Presidency against an incumbent, at another very favourable time for Democrats, in the aftermath of Richard Nixon's resignation and in the midst of the 1970s stagflation. In office, however, Carter struggled to formulate a clear response to the economic problems which the US and the global economy faced. He was a micromanager and failed to articulate a broader vision, and he also suffered foreign policy reverses, particularly those flowing from a new Russian assertiveness, and from the Iranian revolution. He lost the 1980 election to Ronald Reagan.

Winning the presidency in a period of economic crisis, even when it can be blamed on the previous administration, is not always a recipe for success. Roosevelt managed to impose his leadership and redefined the nature of American politics, but as the example of Carter demonstrates, it is also possible for a new president to be swamped by the pressures which the recession brings, fail to make an impact and be a one-term president, ceding the political and ideological initiative to others. Roosevelt did not know when he was elected that he wanted to create the New Deal. In his election address he was still committed to balancing the budget. But he had the political strength and single-mindedness once in office to react to the situation as he found it and to craft a new programme. Obama has a great opportunity but success is far from guaranteed and, given the scale of the problems he faces and the height of the expectations he has generated, failure is more likely than success. Some of his early moves, such as the choice of his economic team, and the fiscal stimulus package passed by Congress in February 2009 lacked a radical edge and attracted criticism for allowing lobbyists to determine where a large part of the money went. The stimulus package attracted little Republican support, allowing the Republicans to disclaim all responsibility for it. One Republican Representative declared before the vote that the only thing the Democrats' stimulus bill would do would be to stimulate more government and more debt. If the recovery programme fails to deliver, the Republicans will return to the attack with a much more aggressive supply-side programme, and will seek to blame Obama and the Democrats in Congress for the continued depressed state of the economy, and for burdening US taxpayers and future US generations with debt. Much depends on whether, like Roosevelt, Obama is able to craft a narrative of the crisis which shapes popular perceptions and arouses popular enthusiasm for the solutions he proposes.

In another major Anglo-American democracy, Britain, the politics of recession left the Labour Government, in its twelfth year of office, fighting for survival at the beginning of 2009. Britain, like the US, was one of the architects of the neo-liberal order, and had possessed in Margaret Thatcher one of its inspirational political leaders. The degree of polarization that existed in Britain in the 1970s and the sharpness of the alternatives meant that Britain was to undergo a more sudden and complete neo-liberal transformation than other European economies. In the eyes of the rest of the world, Britain and America were the main authors of the policies associated with the Washington consensus, and Anglo-Saxon capitalism became a term both of analysis and of disparagement by critics of the financial growth model through the 1990s.

So powerful was the neo-liberal order, and so successful were the Anglo-Saxon economies during the 1990s, that other countries had to accommodate to it, and within the heartland states, domestic oppositions had to do the same. In Britain this took the form of the reinvention of the

Labour Party as New Labour, a party that was now pro-business and pro-market in much more unambiguous ways than the old Labour Party had been, and moreover a party now committed to working within the constraints of neo-liberalism. After the recession of the 1990s and Britain's forced departure from the Exchange Rate Mechanism in 1992, in effect a devaluation, the British economy began to perform strongly and entered into a period of steady unspectacular but nevertheless cumulatively impressive growth which lasted sixteen years, only finally being interrupted in 2008. This was the longest period of sustained growth in Britain's modern economic history and contrasted sharply with the much more uneven economic performance between 1918 and 1992.

Labour won the 1997 general election and therefore was in office for most of this period of sustained growth, and was quick to claim the credit for it, although the trajectory had already been set under John Major and Kenneth Clarke. Labour, however, consolidated the new model which the Conservatives had created. It was recognizably a neo-liberal growth model, and Labour sought to embed it and enhance its own credibility with the markets by giving the Bank of England formal responsibility for setting interest rates, and adopting clear fiscal rules for managing the budget and public debt. Labour also gave a pledge not to increase income taxes, and it continued with the Conservatives' regulatory reforms of the financial sector, and the drive for better public services. Labour developed the notion of a social investment state and, after at first rigidly adhering to Conservative spending targets, began to increase public spending substantially. On the back of this success Labour won three consecutive terms of office, much the longest period of success the party had had since its foundation.

Since Labour was so strongly associated with the period of boom and its accompanying bubbles, in particular the huge rise in house prices, the bursting of the bubble and the financial collapse in 2007–8 hurt Labour, as the incumbent, severely. At the end of 2007 and during the first nine months of 2008 the party appeared to be heading for inevitable defeat under its new leader, Gordon Brown. The ratings of both the party and Gordon Brown himself sank to very low levels, and the Conservatives for the first time since before 1992 soared in the polls, and they were regarded as certain to win the next election. The politics of recession can be fickle, however, and when the crash struck in September 2008, Labour and Gordon Brown were unexpectedly able to turn the situation to their advantage. Brown appeared much happier focusing on a major financial crash, and was both decisive in preventing the collapse of major banks and in giving a lead to efforts at international coordination. His ratings and that of the Labour Party improved for a time, while the Conservatives declined, although they remained in the lead. The incumbent in this case benefited more, at first, from the crisis than the challenger. But once the effects of the recession began to be felt, the unpopularity of the government returned. Labour had hauled itself back into contention, as a result of its response to the September crash, but in January 2009 the worsening news about jobs and output, and the IMF prediction that the UK economy would contract more than any other advanced economy in 2009, made its task seem all but impossible. The party had been in office for almost twelve years, and could hardly disclaim responsibility for regulatory failures, or for the enthusiasm with which Labour ministers, and particularly Gordon Brown, had celebrated the success of the City. The close links between ministers and bankers made them seem part of the same political class and the target of increasing public anger.

The Conservatives adroitly did what they could to fan this mood, suggesting that the excesses of the boom were directly attributable to the lax regulation which Labour ministers had overseen, and that the failure to sort the mess out was due to incompetence and timidity. Yet part of the problem for the Conservatives as the main opposition was that, like the Republicans in the US, they were even more closely identified in the public mind with the financial boom and with deregulation. Up until the crisis broke they had been pressing for still further relaxations on financial regulation in order to preserve and extend London as an international financial centre. The Conservatives and the City of London were hard to disentangle. The Anglican Church had once been described as the Tory party at prayer, and Hilaire Belloc had always viewed the City as the Tory party at lunch. Since the Thatcher years and the Big Bang, however, the City seemed to have become the Tory party at work. The two merged seamlessly into one another.

David Cameron became the leader of the Conservatives after the party's unprecedented third consecutive election defeat to Labour in 2005. His strategy was to adopt aspects of New Labour's strategy in the 1990s, positioning the party as a centrist party, slightly to the left of the government on many issues, such as the environment and civil liberties. When the crisis struck it was difficult at first for the Conservatives to disengage from this strategy. All their policies assumed continuing growth, so that they would be able to take a growth dividend, honouring Labour's spending pledges, but still finding some room to cut taxes. The disappearance of any prospect of growth left the Conservatives for a while without any clear strategy for the looming recession, and they suffered from the comparison with the government's conviction of what should be done, and its energy in prosecuting it. This began to change, however, once the Conservatives began to develop a new narrative of Labour failure, connecting the 2008 financial crisis with earlier financial crises when Labour had been in office, 1976 and 1931 in particular, and seeking to lump regulators, ministers and bankers together as an elite which had failed and which should be held to account.

The British case showed all too clearly the perils of incumbency. The Labour government had been in office too long by 2009 to escape blame, and it was too flatfooted and too timid in its response to the crisis. It still hoped that the financial system in which it had reposed such trust would recover and sort things out. That is why it encouraged Lloyds Bank to take over HBOS in September 2008, rather than simply nationalizing HBOS. The scale of the losses HBOS was subsequently to announce in February 2009 cast doubt on the wisdom of the government's earlier decisions. When the government did start to act, its flurry of initiatives in late 2008 were dismissed as having little effect, and being muddled. The opposition parties argued that even if some of the policies were right, the government had no idea of how to implement them. The promises the government made to protect its citizens seemed empty when set against the rapid increases in unemployment, and growing public awareness of the debt burdens the government was incurring to shore up the banks (£600 billion by one estimate). What this implied for future tax rises and public expenditure cuts created an increasingly angry and unforgiving mood. The deepening recession at the beginning of 2009 led to rapid increases in unemployment and demands for protection. The unofficial strikes in January 2009 over the employment by TOTAL of Italian workers to build a new oil terminal threw back at Gordon Brown the promise he had made of 'British jobs for British workers' at the Labour Party conference in 2007. The government was not willing to embrace protectionism, but it had few ways it could be seen to be protecting its citizens from the storm that was now brewing.

Right and Left

There is a wider question, irrespective of incumbency, about whether recessions in the long run favour the right or the left. There is an inherent vagueness about these terms, yet they are continually in public discourse. The simplest spectrum which defines right and left is the role of the state in the economy, with those on the right favouring market solutions and those on the left favouring state intervention. But it is complicated by other spectrums of left and right, such as the spectrum of attitudes towards equality and inequality. Obama would be placed on the left spectrum on both equality and state intervention, but he is determined to govern as a pragmatic centrist, as shown by the selection of his Cabinet.

Neo-liberalism, although not originally a doctrine of the right, has become associated more with the right than with the left in the last three decades. That could mean that politicians of the left and centre are likely to benefit in this recession, from a popular instinct that true believers in neo-liberalism are not much interested in the security of ordinary citizens in times of hardship. Politicians of the left generally still possess a rhetoric of intervention to advance security and welfare. Recessions are great breeders of insecurity – about houses, jobs, investments, and pensions. In populations as highly leveraged as Britain and the United States any check to expansion can produce a surge of fear, because most people in these societies have no significant assets, and no way to protect themselves from the effects of recession. Roosevelt turned out to be such a dominant president because he understood the times. When he said in his Inaugural Address, 'You have nothing to fear but fear itself', he was speaking directly to the wave of fear that was sweeping America, and urging people to trust him to do something about it. Many Americans at that time had much more to fear than just fear itself, but Roosevelt was able to suggest that he had some answers to the problems that people faced. Recessions, in this way, give great opportunities to the left but politicians have to be very bold in seizing them, and constructing narratives of the crisis that are popular and plausible, and suggest radical solutions. They must also be prepared to face great opposition, as Roosevelt did.

In most past recessions the political fallout has in fact seldom favoured parties and leaders of the left. Parties and leaders of the right have generally been much more adept at seizing the initiative, and framing the narrative in ways which favour them. The New Deal in the United States was a rare exception. In Britain and other parts of Europe the economic and financial collapse did not bring many left-wing regimes to power. In Britain the crisis destroyed the minority Labour Government of Ramsay Macdonald when the Cabinet could not agree to budget cuts which would have meant cutting the meagre dole payments to the unemployed. When the Cabinet split on the issue, Macdonald was persuaded by the King to form a National Government, embracing the Conservatives, some of the Liberals and a small number of Labour MPs. This National Government, which was really a Conservative Government under another name, stayed in power throughout the 1930s. The main objective for which it had been formed was not achieved. When it imposed the cuts the Labour Government had refused to implement, Navy ratings mutinied at Invergordon, in protest at the reduction in their pay. This was the final blow for the pound. The resulting collapse forced the suspension of the gold standard, and ushered in a very different economic policy for coping with the depression.

Elsewhere in Europe developments rarely favoured the left. Sweden was the big exception, where a Social Democratic Government was elected in 1932 and was to rule uninterruptedly until the 1970s. In Germany unemployment rose dramatically from two to six million as industrial production fell by 42 per cent, and as the electorate polarized between the National Socialists and the Communists, the Conservative parties and key figures in the German establishment allowed Hitler to become Chancellor and take control of the government, giving birth to the Third Reich. In France popular front government was short-lived and for most of the 1930s the right dominated. Spain did swing left but the Republican Government was overthrown by a right-wing military uprising under Franco. Italy remained firmly under the grip of the Fascists and Mussolini. Elsewhere, the depression was the occasion for the Japanese military to seize control of the Emperor and the government. China was wracked by civil war and external incursions. Much of the rest of the world was still incorporated within European colonial empires. Only Russia was taking a different path at this time, isolated from the western capitalist economy, and embarking on the five-year plans and the Great Terror. Many people growing up in Europe and America in the 1930s concluded that the future would be decided by a war to the death between fascism and communism. There seemed little room for progressive politics or middle ways. The general impact of the politics in the recession in the 1930s was a move to the right, and in many cases to the far right. In a major crisis market failure is often immense, but government failure is also often immense. Governments can never respond quickly enough, because the bureaucratic coordination is generally slow and cumbersome, so there is a mismatch between rhetoric and what actually happens on the ground. The United States was exceptional, as so often before and since.

In the 1970s stagflation the degree of polarization was less extreme than in the 1930s, but again the general movement was to the right rather than the left. The communist world was much larger in the 1970s than it had been in the 1930s, including as it did China, parts of South East Asia, as well as the Soviet Union and much of eastern and central Europe. It had its own problems but it was largely insulated from the problems of the western capitalist economy. During the 1970s there were left of centre administrations elected in the US, in Britain and in West Germany, but all three eventually gave way to right of centre governments in the 1980s, and in the case of Britain and the US to radical right of centre governments. Spain and France went the other way, electing Conservative governments in the 1970s and socialist governments in the 1980s, but, after the brief flirtation with socialist measures, the Mitterrand Government was forced to change tack. With the exception of a few states, the 1970s was not a great time for left of centre government. The parties of the right appeared to have a better grasp of the nature of the crisis and what needed to be done to put it right. Here the pivotal role played by the United States in the global economy was important. Once America moved right to resolve the crisis, other countries were forced to adapt to that reality. In the 1930s the breakdown of the international financial system and the liberal world order meant that each country developed its own strategy for survival, often unrelated to those elsewhere. The American New Deal was influential in retrospect but less so at the time. Other countries, like Germany, developed their own New Deal but the content and the politics were very different from the United States.

The current recession will be different again. Some leading countries, like Canada, appear relatively insulated from the crisis because of the more prudent nature of their banking system. Others will be much harder hit. The international financial system and the American world order are still intact, and therefore what happens in the United States politically will have a major influence on developments elsewhere. But there are many other variables in play. Communism has collapsed as an autarchic system outside the capitalist world economy; the world has been reunified but this means there are once again several distinct groupings and centres of power. The United States can no longer dominate as it once did. Its capacities are still immense, but in relative terms it is weaker. The EU, Japan, China, India, Brazil and Russia are now all important players. This crisis is a global crisis more than at any time before. Its implications are explored in the next chapter.

In past crises of capitalism the political forces that benefit have often not been those of the left. Paradoxically, the left has most often been strong when the economy is strong, and weak when it is weak. Socialists in the past had often entertained a millennial view of a great crisis which would shake capitalism to its foundations, lift the scales from the eyes of the workers and make apparent the urgency of replacing capitalism with an alternative economic system. Capitalist crises have never worked out like that, mainly because a crisis is a moment of danger and insecurity, a leap in the dark. Once people are fearful, they will tend to seek security from whoever can offer it. Crises are not good times for optimism and hope. Obama may be fortunate that his campaign for president took place before the full force of the recession hit. In a crisis people crave reassurance and authority rather than radicalism and they punish incompetence. Parties of the right have often shown that they understand the need of individuals for security better than parties of the left.

The parties of the right that succeeded in the Great Depression did so by protecting their citizens. In Britain the Conservatives, who were much the largest part of the 1931 National Government, quickly accepted the suspension of the gold standard and the need to break with free trade, imposing tariffs and giving preference to trade with countries in the Empire, such as Canada. Some of the economic liberals in the government, including Philip Snowden, the former Labour Chancellor of the Exchequer, resigned in protest. This left the Conservative majority free to bring in imperial preference, imposing tariffs on all goods originating outside the British Empire, and a range of other measures to ensure that British citizens were protected. Characteristic of the politics of the time was the legislation to give protection to particular self-employed groups, such as grocers, taxi drivers and newsagents. These were all groups being targeted by the British Union of Fascists, and the Conservatives took care by limiting competition to ensure that they could continue to earn a reasonable living through the depression. Much of industry was reorganized into cartels, and price fixing and other anti-competitive practices were tolerated. The priority as far as the Conservative Government was concerned was to protect the standard of living of the middle class. The burden of adjustment was shifted to sections of the working class in the depressed industrial areas, but other parts of the economy, particularly around London and the South East, began to show substantial growth.

The Nazi regime in Germany also made economic security a priority. Under the guidance of Hjalmar Schacht, who served as Hitler's Finance

Minister, Germany embarked on a massive programme of state investment in roads, housing and the military. Profitability in German industry was quickly restored and the economy boomed in the 1930s, approaching full employment by 1938 and showing signs of severe overheating and rising inflationary pressures. The legitimacy of the regime owed much to its successful economic policy, and to bringing Germany out of the pit into which it had fallen in 1932. Keynes recognized the success of the German policy in the foreword he contributed to the German edition of *The General Theory of Employment, Interest and Money.* Germany revealed the power of the modern state to intervene successfully to shape economic development. Hitler was able to achieve more than Roosevelt in this respect, partly because he did not have local opposition to deal with.

In the 1970s and 1980s it was again parties of the right that were most successful in constructing narratives of the crisis that put the blame for the state of the economy on government intervention and militant trade unions, and offered novel solutions that ultimately crafted the radical restructuring of capitalism along neo-liberal lines in the 1980s, laying the foundations for the bubble economy of the 1990s. The United States as the world's leading economy has been responsible, therefore, for the two major reconstructions of capitalism that led to two extended periods of economic expansion of the global economy under American leadership – the New Deal programme of the 1930s and the neo-liberal programme of the 1980s. If the crash of 2008 and the recession of 2009 do turn out to be part of a broader capitalist crisis, the question is whether it will lead to a further reconstruction of capitalism under American leadership. What happens in the US remains of more importance in this regard than what happens elsewhere. The fact that there are as yet no clear alternative narratives and no very clear ideas of what to do may not matter. There was no clear alternative in the 1930s. *The General Theory* was not published until 1936. Roosevelt's pragmatism found solutions which pointed in a new direction. But the New Deal was not enough. By itself, it did not pull the United States out of depression. Only the Second World War did that. The United States was a rising power in 1933. It is no longer that in 2009. The reconstruction of global capitalism may therefore be more limited than in the two earlier examples, and much will depend on the impact of the crisis on the rest of the world, particularly in Asia, and how countries there respond.

5

The Global Impact

The global financial crisis has profound implications not just for economies and states in one region but across the whole world. The degree of interdependence of this world has been disputed; if global is taken to mean unified, there is much in the global economy that is not truly global. As a process globalization is at best very uneven and incomplete, whether we take trade flows, investment flows, or migrant flows. There is not a single economy even within the United States, still less so in the EU, or Asia, or Africa. The global economy is made up of a multitude of national and regional economies which have established an increasing number of connections between them, and are increasingly subject to multiple and overlapping jurisdictions. On several measures the world is more homogeneous than it once was, but heterogeneity still flourishes, particularly in politics. The trend towards a unified world economy which has been proceeding now for three hundred years is much more advanced than the drive to create a unified jurisdiction to match it. But the degree of integration that has occurred means that there is now almost no community anywhere in the world which is not affected by what happens in other parts of the global economy. The financial crisis is global not because it is the same throughout the world, but because no country can entirely escape it. Some countries are at the centre of the storm, others quite marginal to it. It is extremely hard, however, so pervasive are the connections between all parts of the global economy, for any community to escape involvement entirely, although the fragmented nature of politics encourages all states to pursue their own interests rather than the common interest. This is true for security, for governance and for political economy.

There is a useful comparison to be made with the Great Crash of 1929 and the subsequent Great Depression of the 1930s. Many historians have pointed out that many parts of the world did not experience the kind of depression that the United States did in the 1930s. The idea that the whole world had a decade of high unemployment, poverty and destitution would be incorrect. Even the United States itself, after unemployment had risen to one quarter of the workforce in 1932, saw a rapid recovery in the 1930s.

Growth rates averaged between 8 and 10 per cent, and unemployment fell. There was a further setback in 1937–8, when unemployment rose again but to nothing like the level in 1932. What the US did not achieve was full employment or the kind of prosperity it had enjoyed in the 1920s. The recovery still had a way to go, and many feared the country was locked into a permanent underemployment equilibrium. As argued in the last chapter, it took the Second World War and rearmament to change that.

The pattern was similarly diverse across other countries. There was no uniform 'Great Depression' experience. What was common to all countries was the context. The breakdown of the international monetary system, the collapse of the gold standard and the end of the attempt pursued since 1918 to try and recreate the political and economic conditions for a restoration of the pre-war liberal order – that was a reality created by the events of 1929–31, and which every country had to respond to in its own way. Despite some international conferences and some talk of cooperation, it was not just collective security which foundered in the 1930s. Collective political economy went down as well. The major countries all pursued national routes to recovery, concentrating on stabilizing their own economies and protecting their own citizens. This was particularly true of Germany, of Britain and, above all, of the United States.

The global impact of the 1929 financial crisis shattered the remaining supports for a liberal international order, and strengthened the protectionist and nationalist impulses which were already strong and now had the opportunity to become much stronger. Contemporaries sensed that the liberal era was finally over and that a world of aggressive power politics was taking its place, a world of regional blocs, separate currencies, high tariff walls, capital controls, tight borders and competition for territory to give access to greater resources and population.

The 1930s has generally been viewed subsequently as a decade that led to catastrophe, the catastrophe of the Second World War. On this standard reading the collapse of the gold standard and the international monetary system and the fragmenting of the world into heavily armed and increasingly hostile regional blocs led down a slippery slope to full armed conflict, with Germany and Japan in different parts of the world seeking to break the stranglehold of Britain, France and the United States and create territorial empires for themselves which would guarantee their world status and world power. But there was nothing inevitable about the descent into world war. There might instead have been an accommodation between the regional blocs that lasted for many decades. In some industries, for example, such as chemicals, an international cartel formed between Germany, Britain and the United States. In a world divided into separate jurisdictions there is always the possibility that rivalry over territory and resources will spill over into war, and wars have been regular occurrences in the international state system. But there have also been long periods of peace and mutual accommodation between states. World government has never been more than a distant possibility, but other alternatives to perpetual war have emerged, including the idea of a liberal world order, in which the tendency to war has been held in check by the growth of interdependence and by the ministrations of a more or less benign hegemonic state. Such orders have not suppressed conflict altogether, but they sometimes limit it and redirect it.

World trade did not disappear during the 1930s, but it declined sharply, by up to 30 per cent between 1930 and 1932, and then recovered slowly for the rest of the decade, but did not return to pre-crisis levels. There were many new obstacles in the path of a rapid expansion of trade, and overall growth for many countries remained subdued. The responses to the crisis had not resolved it. There were few signs of a return to greater integration and cooperation in the global economy. A different model was now dominant, but one that demonstrated that it was capable of delivering growth and considerable prosperity and stability for the different national economies, and many assumed that this would be the norm from now on. Liberalism came to seem an interlude in the development of the international political economy and the international state system, brought about by a particular conjunction of circumstances in the nineteenth century, and the accident of the role Britain was able to play in the global economy, a role which in the 1930s could not be restored.

If comparison is made with the 1970s stagflation, as the second great global capitalist crisis of the twentieth century, the picture is rather different. There was once again a major crisis of the international monetary system, which led to the decision to suspend convertibility of the dollar and in effect to break up the Bretton Woods system, which had only properly functioned for about thirteen years. A regime of floating exchange rates took its place. The oil price shocks triggered a global recession, and unemployment rose steeply, but the problem that governments faced was not deflation but accelerating inflation, combined with low or non-existent growth. The United States, as the dominant power and leading architect of the post-war financial and economic order, was not displaced or sidelined in the way that Britain was in the 1930s. It took the lead in reshaping the financial and economic order to fit better with its interests. The 1970s and early 1980s were a period of restructuring which laid the foundations for the triumphant reassertion of American interests and American power in the 1990s. There was talk in the 1970s of the western economy breaking up into regional blocs based on Japan, the EU and the US, but in retrospect this was never very likely. The EU and Japan were firmly tied into the security alliances with the US, they were economically dependent on the US, and there was no significant political will to challenge the US, or any significant US intention to disengage.

What the 1970s stagflation did highlight was the extent to which the gap had closed between the United States, on the one hand, and other capitalist economies, notably Japan and Germany, on the other. But their challenge was clearly quite unlike the challenge they offered in the 1930s. They were now firmly within the liberal economic order and had no intention of breaking it up. For all the difficulties of the 1970s, the capitalist world stayed together, helped in part by the perception of a continuing external security threat from the Soviet Union and its allies. It was unthinkable in security terms for the United States in the 1970s to abandon the liberal economic order it had done so much to create. Security issues and political economy issues were bound very closely together in American thinking throughout the Cold War period, and this ensured that, although there was a new direction after the crisis, there was also a great deal of continuity. The 1970s stagflation produced a major evolution of the US-dominated system, but not a major break with it. The impact of the crisis on the rest of the world reflected that key fact.

The global impact of the 2008 financial crash and the 2009 recession will be different from both the 1930s and 1970s. It matters a great deal, however, which in the end it more resembles. Will it produce a major break in the structure of the post-war order, with the displacement of the United States from its leading role, or will the United States continue in that role, although possibly with a new emphasis and direction? In the 1930s isolationism was extremely strong in the United States, and many initiatives of the Congress, including the Smoot-Hawley Tariff passed in 1930 which quadrupled many existing tariff rates, as well as the priorities of the Roosevelt administration, reflected this. Even after the Second World War there were strong isolationist tendencies still at work, represented, for example, by Senator Robert Taft, who had been strongly opposed to American involvement in the Second World War before the attack on Pearl Harbor, and only narrowly lost the Republican nomination in 1952 to

Eisenhower. The ascendancy of the liberal internationalists under Eisenhower was not inevitable.

As in all crises, there is nothing certain about how the present one will be resolved, how long it will last, or what the fallout will be. As events unfolded in 2008 it was obvious that there were risks to the future of the multilateral trading order, and question marks over globalization itself. The talk of 'deglobalization', which surfaced at the Davos conference in January 2009, was a little premature, but the longer the crisis lasts the more likely it is to dispel some of the myths of the hyper-globalists by bringing into greater prominence the national and regional foundations of the global economy. But that is not the same as forecasting the breaking up of the existing forms of this global economy. Protectionist pressures were evident in 2008, and had been developing for some time. Some countries, including South Korea, had begun to impose higher tariffs; many others were considering it. Such moves can spread rapidly and force other countries into taking steps to protect their industries. The enthusiasm of the US Congress for adding 'Buy America' clauses to the Obama administration's stimulus package, most of which were stripped out before the bill became law, is a pointer to what could happen. The failure in 2008 of the Doha Round of trade negotiations organized by the WTO makes a slide into protectionism in current circumstances more likely, but still not inevitable. Supporters of open trade fear that if countries are hurt badly enough by the global recession, they may look for ways to protect themselves from the worst effects, even while acknowledging the long-term problems which this may create for them if every other country does the same.

What will also be watched for closely will be any moves by states to detach themselves or insulate themselves from the international monetary system, by making their currencies inconvertible or by imposing capital controls. The international agencies backed by the United States have put great pressure on countries to accept full currency convertibility and to scrap capital controls, and this has exposed countries to the effects of the financial turmoil in America and Europe. Some countries, notably China, have joined the WTO and engaged fully in trade, but have kept control of their currency. China is unlikely to give up that control in the midst of this crisis, and other countries may be tempted to follow its example. The liberal order that the United States promoted through the 1980s and 1990s now faces a severe test. Does it still offer sufficient advantages for countries to want to remain within it?

The global financial crisis not only highlights the national and regional foundations of the global economy, and encourages states to take steps to protect their citizens as best they can; it also shines a sharp light on the structural imbalances of the global economy, which grew up during the boom and were not corrected. One of these imbalances was the distribution of surpluses and deficits within the global economy. The exports of some countries, including Germany and China, rocketed during the boom and resulted in huge financial surpluses, while other countries, including the United States, racked up vast deficits on their current account. The surpluses recycled through the financial system and helped to create the credit boom in the deficit countries which allowed them to go on spending and borrowing. The global economy lacked effective mechanisms to redistribute the surpluses. When the crash came it affected not only the deficit countries but the surplus countries too, because their markets disappeared.

A second structural imbalance was the inequality in the distribution of income and wealth. There was some change in the number of the world's population classified as poor during the boom, largely because of the improvement of China and India from a very low base, but in absolute terms the problem of poverty became ever more grotesque, because of the contrast between the excesses of consumption in rich countries with the poverty in poor countries. At the millennium the UN calculated that there were still one billion people earning only a dollar a day or less, and another two billion earning only two dollars a day. These imbalances were most stark on a global level, but also existed within the rich countries themselves, in several of which, including Britain and the United States, there had been a marked trend towards growing inequality from the late 1980s.

A third structural imbalance was the dependence of different parts of the global economy on essential resources such as water, oil and metals compared to their ease of access to these resources. All three imbalances contribute in the short term to tension and conflict, and are hard to deal with in the circumstances of a recession. They are hard enough to deal with in times of rapid growth. A reconstruction of the global economy to make possible a new phase of growth would need to begin tackling these imbalances, but achieving that will not be simple, since it requires agreement on a new set of rules, which would require a set of political compromises between the world's leading economies. The United States is best placed to take the lead in brokering such deals, but whether the United States will see it as in its interest to do so, or even to make the attempt, is unclear. One of the main issues in any such negotiations, as Russia and China have already made clear, would be the exclusive reserve currency status of the dollar. In a world of fluctuating exchange rates, and huge financial losses suffered by so many countries as a result of the financial crash, and the denomination of many of their assets in dollars, major changes are indispensable if a more stable financial order to allow a recovery of world trade and growth is to be created. But agreeing them is a huge task.

The Role of the United States

In determining what the global impact of the crash and the recession is likely to be, the role which the United States chooses to play will be crucial. There is a danger of focusing too much on the United States, as though only American attitudes and policies mattered. That is obviously not the case, and particularly not in this crisis. Yet the United States is still of major importance for two reasons. First, it still has structural capacities in several different fields which continue to make it the world's dominant power and, second, the crisis first arose in the United States, and reflects crucial aspects of its economy and policy as it has developed in the last twenty-five years. Since the United States still comprises around 25 per cent of the global economy, this makes understanding the dynamics of the crisis within the US essential for assessing its wider impact. The response of the United States was crucial for the way in which the last crisis in the global economy, the 1970s stagflation, was resolved, and the conditions created for the second boom since 1945 under US auspices, although one with much less secure foundations than the first. The question is whether the US can now create the conditions for a third boom, a third era of US dominance, or whether this can only now be done in concert with others.

One of the key contexts for understanding the impact of this crisis on the United States is the role the US has played within the international state system. During the 1980s there was a major debate about American decline, and whether the bases of the dominant position which the US had occupied both in the international state system and in the global economy were being eroded. This debate reflected the setbacks which the United States had experienced in the 1970s, particularly the collapse of Bretton Woods, the loss of Vietnam and the global recession. Some of the critics of the idea of American decline, such as Susan Strange, argued that what was being ignored was the way in which the crisis of the 1970s, far from enfeebling the United States, had allowed it to develop a new financial growth model, to strengthen its military and to reorganize its alliances and its policies, and that a new period of US dominance was about to dawn. The opening of the Berlin Wall and the collapse of the Soviet Union were the moments which signalled this rebirth, but the conditions for it were laid down in response to the crisis of the 1970s.

What characterized the United States for a time after 1991 was that it possessed overwhelming military force, and lacked any serious military rival or challenger. So advanced and preponderant were the equipment and techniques of the US military that resistance to it in any kind of conventional warfare seemed futile. The position of the United States was further enhanced by its network of more than 700 bases across the world, and its deployment of more than 1.5 million military personnel overseas. After the demise of the Soviet Union, the United States was estimated to spend ten times as much as any other country on its military. In 2008 it accounted for half of all the military expenditures in the world, and within the NATO alliance for 71 per cent.

The weakness of the United States' position was that, while no other state could stand against it militarily, the cost of maintaining its military and the overseas bases around the world was very high, and the United States no longer had the same economic or financial strength which it had enjoyed in the past. The United States was still the largest economy in the world by some margin in 2008, at $13 trillion three times as large as Japan, the second largest economy. But the EU taken together was by now as large as the US, and China and India were growing rapidly and closing the gap. The United States had also long ceased to be a country in financial surplus, and had become very dependent on overseas lenders (see Table 5.1).

Table 5.1   US Federal debt to selected foreign countries (in $ billion and percentages)

Country	2002 ($ billion)	2002 %	2007 ($ billion)	2007 %
Japan	378	31	581	24
China	118	10	478	20
UK	80	7	157	7
Oil Exporters	50	4	138	6

Source: data from Congressional Research Service, *Foreign Holdings of Federal Debt*, March 2008.

American growth had become very dependent on boosting consumer debt and funding the deficits through borrowing from China, the Middle East and Japan. Reagan had come to office promising to balance the budget, but had massively increased the deficit. The dollar remained the main international currency, the currency which was used as the reserve currency by most of the rest of the world, and in which a great deal of the world's trade was still conducted. But the basis of this financial predominance was no longer so clearly the industrial strength, productivity and growth potential of the US economy. Becoming a persistent debtor country is an uncomfortable position for the United States, since it allows other states, like China and some of the Middle East states, to use their Sovereign Wealth Funds to purchase US assets cheaply. The persistent long-term fall in the dollar has also meant a gradual diversification out of the dollar towards other currencies, because of the costs for other countries of continuing to hold a great deal of their assets in dollars. The financial crisis may accelerate this trend. With interest rates in the US brought down practically to zero at the end of 2008, the attractiveness of holding dollars was not obvious. The financial and industrial weakness of the United States was disguised during the boom of the 1990s. There were several bubbles and financial crises during this time, but none of them seemed to threaten the continued prosperity of the United States. American banks and investors became adept at creating financial bubbles in particular markets and particular currencies, then collapsing them, making enormous profits in the process. The speculation against sterling in 1992 which forced Britain out of the European Exchange Rate Mechanism was an example of this; so was the East Asian financial crisis of 1997, and the dot.com bubble of 2000. The power of financial capital had been unleashed by the deregulatory moves of the 1980s, and the imposition of free trade rules on the rest of the world. The housing market bubble in 2002–7 was expected to be just another of these bubbles, which would be blown up and then collapsed, without long-term damage to the financial system, but at huge profits to its leading players, the losses being distributed to weaker players in the game. The US investment banks based in New York and London learned to surf the financial waves of this bubble economy. Employment was high, inflation low and, provided the emerging economies continued to grow rapidly and provided an unending supply of cheap products and financial savings to support the economies of the United States and Europe, it was assumed this could continue indefinitely. A way had been found to make growth everlasting, and to allow the banks to make super-profits.

The collapse of this growth model and the ideologies and politics which underpinned it has highlighted the serious weaknesses in the economic position of the United States. Rebuilding its position will not be easy, since it still seeks to spend as much as ever on its military and overseas bases, and its domestic economy is in serious trouble. There are mounting tensions in the US brought about by increasing unemployment and stagnant wages. Although the last two decades have been very good for some Americans, for the majority real wages have barely risen at all. The self-image of Americans that every generation is better off than the previous generation has been challenged. To the extent that living standards have continued to advance it has been through the piling up of debt. The unwinding of the debt mountain is likely to point up just how small have been the gains of the previous twenty years. The real incomes of many Americans will be cut.

What options exist for the United States in this situation? Three main alternatives have been canvassed. The impact of the crisis could force the US to turn inwards, disengaging from the rest of the world, reducing its military presence overseas and its interventions, as well as becoming more protectionist and autarchic in its economic policy. Such a policy could be very popular within the United States itself, and it plays to the old American yearning not to get entangled in the affairs of the rest of the world, but it would mark a major break with the policies of engagement and leadership and the projection of American power around the globe which have guided US policy since the 1940s.

A second alternative would be a renewed attempt to pursue the doctrines of American primacy and unilateralism which characterized the Bush presidency, while trying to avoid some of the mistakes. This policy would emphasize US dominance and would assert American interests, and would not seek to rebuild bridges with allies or use American soft power. The US would be aggressive to many other countries, seeking only coalitions of the willing to pursue its goals, and disengaging from those bodies, including the UN, and possibly even NATO, which no longer seemed fit for purpose. This would be an Anglosphere policy, accepting that American dominance could not be fully restored, but seeking to ensure that America remained the largest and most powerful bloc in the global economy. The countries linked to America would form a network of countries that shared similar values and interests to the United States. The goal of creating an overarching international community would be abandoned.

A third alternative is a revived multilateralism, through which the United States would seek to re-engage with all major players in the international community, rebuilding international institutions and helping to construct new ones to take account of altered realities. A new readiness to share burdens and to develop cooperative solutions to the many problems facing the world would come to the fore. Given the weakened position of the United States within the global economy, such a policy would need to be aware of the reality of US decline and the difficulty, therefore, of leading in the old way. There would have to be a great deal of patient diplomacy and re-evaluation of American options for this to work, and it would clash with the domestic perception of America's rightful position in the world. Nevertheless, with the election of Barack Obama in 2008, it is this option, the renewal of American leadership but on a new basis, which looks to be the option that will be tried first. A great deal rides on it.

The Role of the EU

The global financial crash has already had a major impact on Europe. The idea at the start of the credit crunch that it would mainly be Anglosphere countries, like Britain and Ireland, with their large financial sectors and deregulated growth models, which would suffer from the downturn, while other European countries would remain largely unaffected, had already proved mistaken by the end of 2008. The reasons are not hard to see. Surplus countries like Germany were very dependent on exports to maintain high levels of employment, and the sharp contraction of demand in the deficit countries had an immediate impact, making Germany one of the first countries to go into recession at the end of 2008. It also became clear that European banks were deeply implicated in the elaborate international financial networks based on London and New York, and had lent heavily.

There are other reasons why Europe cannot escape the global impact of the crisis. The EU may have an economy as large as that of the US, but it is not a state and, although it has integrated some functions and promoted interdependence, it is still far from being an effective actor in foreign and defence policy, or in many economic areas. For some observers it is the continuing subordination of the EU to the US which is one of the most striking features of international politics in the last twenty years. The much publicized tensions between them has not enabled Europe to unite around common policies. Rather they have helped the United States to divide

Europe against itself, a stratagem highlighted by the attack of a leading member of the Bush Administration, Donald Rumsfeld, on 'Old Europe' during the Iraq war.

The EU remains seriously divided over the desirability and the content of a common foreign and defence policy. Two of its members are nuclear powers with significant conventional armed forces, but other member states have neutralism written into their constitutions, or are restricted as to how they may deploy troops abroad. The aspiration of the EU to be a 'civilian power', which projects a different kind of power around the world, a form of soft power, has made some progress and has had some successes, notably in setting down criteria which all states seeking to join the EU must meet. It has been less successful in the Middle East. But the lack of effective hard power or a means to develop a coherent European foreign policy means that several of the larger states pursue their own foreign and defence policies, often weakly coordinated with the EU. In practice, whatever the rhetoric, the EU has continued to rely on US military protection, and has not seriously attempted to take over this role. Substantial US forces remain stationed in Europe, and there are no plans for Europe to take on the burden of its own defence.

The global financial crisis may force a rethink. The US itself may question the cost of its bases in Europe, and the need for them. It may question the value of NATO. In either of the first two scenarios sketched above the crisis could bring a major shift in relationships between Europe and the US. But even if this were to take place, and the election of Obama makes it unlikely, there is still no guarantee that the EU would change very much, or would be able to put together a coherent foreign and defence policy. The interests within the EU are too divergent, and there is no mechanism by which the strongest nations can impose their will on the rest.

The situation is similar in political economy. The global financial crisis might seem an opportunity for the European social model and the eurozone to come into their own. The European growth model and the European social model are distinctly different from the Anglo-American models, and it might be thought, therefore, that they would be relatively free from contagion. Unfortunately for the European economy this does not appear to be the case. The secondary waves from the credit crunch in America have devastated European banking. Major banks like Fortis have had to be rescued, and the same liquidity problems and the accumulation of toxic debts have been revealed in European banks. It appears that European bankers took advantage of the enterprise of New York and

London to take big stakes in the new financial instruments and the new opportunities to get rich fast, earning more than the market average. The recession began to spread rapidly through Europe at the end of 2008, with unemployment climbing steeply and a similar wave of bankruptcies and unemployment as had been observed in the United States. The IMF World Economic Outlook in January 2009 expected the American economy to be less severely hit by the downturn, and to recover more quickly.

With the dollar weakening, and the unhappiness of overseas investors at the size of US deficits, and the potential devaluing of their holdings, it might be thought that the euro would be well placed to become an alternative reserve currency. There are some signs of this occurring, but the euro itself has serious structural flaws which may prevent it from becoming a serious alternative to the dollar. The euro is a monetary union without a fiscal union, which means there is no political authority standing behind it in the way in which the US Treasury and the US Federal Reserve stand behind the dollar. Just how important that can be is shown by the events of 2008. If a crisis of similar magnitude occurred in the Eurozone it is far from clear how the European Central Bank would cope, whether the member governments could agree quickly enough on emergency rescue measures. Similar concerns have been expressed over the ability of the eurozone to hold together through a long recession, when the position of different national economies and, therefore, their economic policy needs are so different. During 2008 severe strains began to emerge in a number of countries, including Ireland, Greece, Portugal, Italy and Spain. In Greece protests against the worsening economic situation, exacerbated by euro membership, erupted into riots. Many European governments may become vulnerable to street protests and populist protests in the next few years, and the European Union may become one of the targets. There are already signs of this happening.

The crisis will therefore be a major test of the eurozone and the ability of this unique monetary experiment to survive. If it does, it will become a rock of stability, and many other countries, including even Britain, may at some point seek entry, or be forced to do for self-protection. But its ability to survive will not be clear for several years, and the political pressures to which it will be subjected will be intense. Survival may well come to depend on the members of the eurozone agreeing some form of fiscal union, to create the capacity to intervene effectively in the economies of the eurozone. But this would be a radical step, and it looked unlikely in 2008, because it would mean the strong countries in the eurozone becoming involved in sorting out the problems in the weaker economies, and developing a common fiscal policy to redistribute resources across the zone.

Another major impact of the crisis on the EU is that it lays bare a series of fault lines which have existed for a long time, but which the political class has preferred to ignore. There is a strong populist revolt in several European countries against the way Europe is run, focusing in particular on the free trade rules of the internal market, which seem to be at variance with the social model established in many of the national economies. The accountability mechanisms in the EU are such that it is very difficult for popular concerns to be represented at the EU level, and this disjunction between the European political class and the European electorate is feeding the disengagement and disillusion which has produced negative votes in referendums on the constitutional treaty held in France, the Netherlands and Ireland. From the perspective of the European social model, Europe has adopted an economic policy which is much closer to the Anglo-American model than it is to the European one. At the European Council in Lisbon in March 2000 a strategy was drawn up with the aim of making the EU the most dynamic and competitive knowledge-based economy in the world, capable of sustainable economic growth with more and better jobs and greater social cohesion, and respect for the environment, by 2010. This became known as the Lisbon process, but progress towards implementing it was modest by the time of the financial crash in 2007–8. It is possible that the impact of the crisis may cause a sharp turn towards re-embedding the European social model, and altering the internal market and the Lisbon process to reflect it. But there are few signs as yet that the European political class is thinking along these lines.

Events may force their hand, but for other reasons the impact of the crisis on Europe may lead to a weakening rather than a strengthening of its position. There are strong concerns over the rate of population increase and over the dynamism and inventiveness of many parts of the European economy, and the quality of its education. Europe is likely to find ways to protect itself in this crisis, but it is unlikely to emerge from it stronger than before. Forging political consensus and political will through the European institutions is just too difficult, and absorbs too much time and energy. The crisis may well confirm the continued decline of Europe, as it shrinks in terms of both population and GDP in relation to the rising economic powers of China, India and Brazil. One of the most profound shifts that this crisis may facilitate is the moment when the world ceases to be Eurocentric, and it is no longer possible to think that it is. Europeans can hardly imagine what that means, they are so used to thinking of Europe as the centre of the world, with the United States as an extension of it. But that may all be about to change.

Japan

Japan remains the second largest economy in the world, but suffered a ten-year deflation in the 1990s. It was one of the first economies to which the term 'credit crunch' was applied, because of the contraction of the supply of bank credit caused by the accumulation of bad debts, loans that could not be repaid, in the financial system. Part of the solution was a massive recapitalization of the banks in 1998–9. After hauling itself back and seeing growth resume at a steady pace after 2000, Japan at first seemed insulated from the effects of the credit crunch in Europe and North America, and during the first half of 2008 was still a significant source of funds for the rest of the international banking industry. This changed after September 2008, when the shock waves from the bank failures across the world caused a stock market crash in Japan and widespread financial panic. The Nikkei share average dropped 24 per cent in October, its biggest ever fall. The trigger for this appears to have been the default by Lehman brothers and Kaupthing, one of the largest Icelandic banks, on yen-denominated Samurai bonds. These bonds had had high credit ratings, and the default sent a very negative signal to the markets. New bond issues had virtually dried up by the end of 2008, and this was causing problems for companies which had relied on the bond markets to raise capital. The banks were reluctant to expand their lending to make up the shortfall, and this was beginning to cause a severe credit squeeze, particularly for smaller companies.

The situation is not comparable to the early 1990s, since Japanese banks have been prudently managed since then and have avoided the accumulation of the large debts that were built up during the 1980s property bubble and then proved so difficult to unwind and offload. They were not sucked into the 1990s bubble economy in the same way that other banks were around the world. Nevertheless, Japan was unable to insulate itself from the effects of the crash, and fears grew during 2008 that Japan might be pushed back into deflation. The IMF predicted a sharper downturn in Japan in 2009, *minus* 2.6 per cent, than in the group of advanced economies as a whole, and Japan also revised down its own economic forecasts. In response to the deteriorating situation, and mindful of the deflationary trap in which the economy was caught in the 1990s, the Bank of Japan cut interest rates drastically during 2008, practically to zero. During the 1990s it had reacted much more cautiously and it had taken eight years from 1991 to 1999 for short-term interest rates to be brought down from 8.3 per cent to zero per cent. Even then the economy was still caught in a liquidity trap. This time the financial authorities were determined to prevent something similar and, in addition to rapidly reducing interest rates, they launched in January 2009 a scheme to take over corporate credit risks by directly buying corporate bonds, planning to absorb around 30 per cent of these bonds into the public sector. This followed an earlier move to lower the credit rating of corporate debt which it would accept as collateral from A to BBB.

The sharpness of the downturn in Japan in the last three months of 2008 brought a very swift response from the authorities, keen to match the US Federal Reserve and to prevent any repetition of the 1990s. The policy adopted again was the one pioneered by the Japanese in 1998–9, now known as quantitative easing; dropping interest rates to zero and flooding the markets with money to avoid a liquidity trap. It worked in 1998–9, but in 2009 it was taking place in a very different global environment in which growth in the rest of the advanced economies had stopped as well, and had decelerated in the emerging economies. The hope was that coordinated action between the central banks would stabilize all the financial markets in the world and allow an early return to growth.

The Rising Economic Powers

For the emerging economies, particularly in Asia, the impact of the financial crash and the global recession is likely to confirm their increasing importance, but it will not leave them unscathed. The Asian financial crisis of 1997 was a setback to several of the most dynamic economies in the region, but they soon bounced back. In retrospect that crisis can be seen as a local bubble within the global economy, which had only a limited effect on the heartlands of this economy in New York and London. The current crisis is right in those heartlands and spreading outwards. No country is immune from it, but many of the emerging economies may survive it in better shape than the established economies of Europe and North America.

Russia in recent years has been lumped in with Brazil, India and China as one of the four key emerging economies, which were given the acronym of the BRICs by Goldman Sachs, but Russia and Brazil are rather different from the other two. Their high growth rates in recent years reflect the boom in the prices of natural resources, with which both countries are well endowed. Russia in particular is placed differently, due to its history, and to its long isolation from the global economy. What makes it an emerging economy is its attempts since the end of communism to become more integrated into the global economy. During the 1990s the economy was in a very bad condition because so much of the plant was obsolete, and the switch to a market economy took place before appropriate institutions had been created. For a time many workers went without pay, and parts of the economy reverted to barter. What has changed Russia's situation is not the emergence of new cutting-edge industries, but the exploitation of its vast natural resources. The commodity price bubbles, particularly the oil and gas bubble created by the boom, gave a major boost to Russian importance and wealth, and bred a new self-confidence and assertiveness, which had been absent in the Yeltsin years.

Russia has been hit hard by the global financial crisis, not so much because of its exposure to the financial markets, but because of the collapse of commodity prices in the face of the recession which began to take hold in the second half of 2008. This has severely shrunk the Russian economy and reduced the main source of state revenues. Despite its military intervention in South Ossetia in August 2008, subsequent events underlined the extent to which Russian prosperity had become bound up with the global economy and Russia's continued access to it. Under Putin it had become clear that a liberal Russia was not in prospect. That possibility had flickered briefly in the 1990s but had never taken hold. Russia has developed its own very distinctive model of both capitalism and democracy, which continue to set it apart from the rest of Europe and from the United States. But it has not moved back to autarchy. Its incorporation within the global economy appears permanent and is unlikely to be reversed. The pro-western phase of Russian policy did not last very long, and Russia once again shows little sign of wanting to imitate the West in its development. Its policy is, however, in favour of openness and engagement, and with the emergence of other non-western countries as significant players Russia has more scope to form alliances with other countries. With its permanent seat on the Security Council, the size of its landmass and its natural resources, Russia cannot be ignored. It has many weaknesses, not least the difficulties of encouraging a more widely based capitalist class, and an entrepreneurial culture, and reversing the demographic decline and tackling its severe health problems and low life expectancy. The effect of the global financial crisis has been to remind the rest of the world of those weaknesses, but also to highlight its continuing underlying strength, based on its importance as a supplier of primary resources, particularly energy. The interruption of gas supplies to Europe in January 2009 caused by the dispute between Russia and the Ukraine was a clear demonstration of that. Russia is in no position to take any leadership role in the global economy, but it has become a player in the way that the Soviet Union never was.

Russia's present political economy cannot survive unless there is sufficient demand from the rest of the world for its natural resources. China's present political economy cannot survive unless it can continue to sell its manufactures to the consumers and businesses of the established economies. The financial collapse in the capitalist heartlands hurts China even more than it does Russia, because its growth model, which has achieved such stunning success in the last twenty years, has been completely dependent on continuously expanding western markets. The fact that most of these markets did continuously grow through the 1990s and through most of the first decade of the twenty-first century, and that China and other countries were able to manufacture extremely cheaply, drawing on an inexhaustible reservoir of labour on the land, became one of the most important factors in sustaining the boom for so long. Some thought that the global economy had stumbled upon a formula that could banish boom and bust, and allow continuous growth, allowing more and more economies to become emerging economies and emulate the success of China and the Asian tigers. There was no doubt about the ability of the emerging countries to perform this role; what cracked was not the rural labour supply, but the ability of the capitalist heartlands to service ever greater mountains of debt. The problem was exacerbated by Chinese policy, in particular its policy of non-convertibility of its currency, its refusal to allow the yuan to appreciate and restrictions it imposed on foreign imports. It was the cheapness of Chinese goods and its willingness to fund US deficits which kept the bubble inflating as long as it did. But the major imbalance lay in the way the boom was funded in the West, and the belief among governments, regulators, and the financial institutions that this process could be managed, and that only minor adjustments and corrections would be needed.

China's problem is that it cannot now afford to stop growing. Just as Russia has become so dependent on the price that energy commands on world markets, so China has become dependent on creating millions of new jobs in its rapidly expanding urban areas. The internal market is developing, but a large part of the demand to keep Chinese factories in business has to come from abroad, so a global recession, particularly a global recession that might be long-lasting, is extremely serious. Already forecasts of Chinese growth have had to be revised downwards. No-one expects China to stop growing, but at the stage of development that China has reached, even a small deceleration of growth can have serious consequences in terms of unemployment, making it impossible to find jobs for the huge population already within the urban areas, let alone the huge population trying to enter. The dangers of major civil unrest make the preservation of high rates of growth a political necessity for the Chinese government.

The impact of the global financial crisis comes at a difficult time in China's development, but the costs of turning away from the path the Chinese leadership has charted in the last twenty years currently look greater than attempting to stay on it. But there are bound to be difficult choices. The relationship between China and the United States has been steadily growing in importance, but the global financial crisis and the global recession will thrust it centre stage. Any prospect of sustaining a relatively open world trading order will depend on cooperation between China and the United States. Both sides need the other, but the relationship will be a difficult one, and the chances of conflicts and even breakdown are real. The huge financial indebtedness of the US, a great deal of it to China, will not make it easy, since many actions the United States has taken and will take to protect itself and its economy, such as slashing interest rates to zero and encouraging the dollar to devalue, directly damage China's interests as a creditor. In 2008 the Chinese were already beginning to express their alarm at the direction of US policy. The United States is so used to the freedom which the status of the dollar as the world's reserve currency gives it to run deficits with impunity that it will take time to get used to a world where it has to act in a much more constrained way. Similarly, the Chinese should be able to survive a short recession in the US and Europe, but if this recession developed into something much larger and more prolonged, then at some point the Chinese could not afford to wait for the recovery, but would have to take steps to accelerate the development of their potentially vast internal market as well as the regional market around them. This must happen eventually in any case, but if it is forced to happen too quickly it may be accompanied by protectionist measures which imply China turning away from the path of increasing integration in the global economy it has followed up to now. It is already the case that only 30 per cent of the exports from the emerging economies, including China, go to the United States and Western Europe. Over half of China's exports go to other emerging economies. Some of the smaller economies like Singapore and Hong Kong, both important financial centres, are very exposed to what is happening in the global financial markets, but the large economies like China can rely to some extent on investment in infrastructure, and switching production from exports to satisfying domestic and regional consumer demand. This is still likely, however, to mean a slower rate of growth. Slower growth has advantages and disadvantages for China. It would ease the inflationary pressures which were rising quite markedly in 2008. But it would make the task of providing sufficient jobs for the rapidly growing urban working force impossible.

China has so far engaged with the global economy on its own terms. Its currency has remained inconvertible, and the Chinese Government retains important levers over economic policy. The openings to internal democracy have been limited, mostly confined to the local level. The main way in which the regime legitimates itself is through nationalism, but this nationalism is not externally aggressive; rather it celebrates China's economic success and cultural achievements. The 2008 Olympics in Beijing, which the Chinese proclaimed as the most successful Olympics ever, set the tone. Apart from Taiwan and Tibet, which the Chinese regard as part of their historical territory, the Chinese make no territorial claims in their region. The pace of their growth, however, makes them obliged to develop a policy of external expansion, as have all the great capitalist powers in the past, partly to provide markets, partly to ensure control over the raw materials and energy which China needs. The emergence, therefore, of China's Africa policy is hardly a surprise. The potential for conflict over resources in particular regions of the world has always been present in international politics, and looks set to intensify. If China fears a general weakening of the international trading order, then it is likely to redouble its efforts to safeguard the supplies it needs directly. The web of alliances and networks which result could exacerbate antagonisms between the big economic players if frameworks are not devised in which such problems can be handled.

The relationship between China and the United States will not be the only important one, however. Several other emerging economies, particularly India, are also set to become major players alongside the established G7 states. Some other countries, particularly in Latin America, including Brazil and Mexico, have also shown signs of establishing themselves as more significant players, although their economies remain very dependent on the United States in the case of Mexico, and very dependent on the export of natural resources in the case of Brazil. Nevertheless, there does appear to be real change under way in the global economy, with the old closed hierarchy of the leading powers which has existed mostly unchanged for a hundred years, through two world wars, a cold war and two major capitalist crises, finally cracking. This global financial crisis of 2008 may mark the moment after which there is no longer any doubt. Everyone has recently become aware of what a massive change is in prospect, a decisive moment in the history of modern times, with the emergence of Asia, including Japan, on equal terms with the traditional heartlands of the West, in Europe, North America and Australasia.

In the short run the impact of the recession on countries like India and Brazil will be negative, in terms of employment and trade. But, like China, they are launched too far now on their new trajectory to turn back, and in responding to this crisis they will find ways to limit the damage to themselves and plan for the recovery. They are likely to be increasingly loud in calling for changes, however, in the way the global economy is ordered and run. There have been many such calls in the past, but this time several of the nations previously excluded have the power to insist on change. The G20, a meeting of finance ministers and central bank governors since 1999, has begun to emerge as a significant forum. It met at heads of government level in November 2008 and April 2009 to discuss the financial crash and the global recession. Apart from the members of the G8 (Canada, France, Germany, Italy, Japan, Russia, the United States and the United Kingdom), the G20 also includes Argentina, Australia, Brazil, China, India, Indonesia, Mexico, Saudi Arabia, South Africa, South Korea, Turkey and a representative of the European Union. The summit in April 2009 was convened to discuss, first, how to coordinate macro-economic actions to revive the global economy, stimulate growth and employment; second, how to reform and improve the operation of the financial sector; and, third, how to reform international financial institutions – the International Monetary Fund, the Financial Stability Forum and the World Bank.

Capitalist crisis will always create moments of danger, and the danger in this case is fairly plain. The global economy and its institutions could disintegrate in the face of the pressures which the global recession will place on every national government. The temptation to resort to protectionism and controls will be extremely strong, and will be fanned by popular movements demanding it. This process had already begun in a small way in 2008 with measures announced by India, Russia and South Korea. Russia imposed tariffs on imports of cars, aimed particularly at Japanese producers, and began considering controls on a wide range of other goods. The more countries turn to autarchic economic policies, the more likely the territorial principle will come to dominate state policy, and the greater risk that closing of borders will lead to greater nationalism and greater militarization, and a rhetoric of external threats. Preserving a degree of openness and cooperation requires both engagement in international institutions and the continued growth of trade and investment. It is when regimes no longer see the pursuit of engagement and openness as being in their interests, or see that the existing international arrangements are hopelessly weighted against them, that alternative courses of action come to be considered.

Reconstructing the international financial architecture will be very hard to accomplish, because if it is to be successful the interests of the newly emerging economies will have to be accommodated. Negotiations are likely to be very lengthy. Time is not exactly in abundant supply, however, because reform is urgently needed to speed the recovery. The longer the global recession lasts, the more serious the potential consequences for the world order. It will expose the fragility of the economic development and the growth models in many countries, and will force changes of direction.

The Global South

For the emerging economies the global financial crisis will impose severe costs but also an opportunity. Many countries in the Global South face only costs. It is true that they have some degree of insulation from the worst effects of the financial collapse, because their credit rating was so poor that they had limited access to the international financial markets, and were not able to borrow large sums. While the heartlands of capitalism were enjoying the feast, a different face was turned to the Global South. Credit was tight and only advanced on strict conditions by the international agencies.

When the financial crisis first became evident in North America and Europe there was some talk that it might not affect Africa. For much of 2008 the forecasts for African growth remained buoyant, with the IMF predicting in April 2008 that Africa was likely to achieve 6.8 per cent growth. Later in that year there was a marked change of sentiment, as it was realized that Africa would also be quite badly affected by the second wave of the financial crisis, and the UN Millennium goals for promoting development and eradicating poverty would be put further out of reach. Even in the stronger economies, such as South Africa, the earlier optimism gave way to considerable gloom and anxiety by the end of 2008. The change in sentiment took place in the autumn of 2008. Up to then, the prevailing view in the markets was that South Africa would not be too badly affected, but it was not able to insulate itself from the crisis the longer it persisted, and in the autumn of 2008 the South African stock market collapsed and the currency fell sharply.

One way in which the crisis was experienced in Africa was through falling asset prices. This exposed how the lack of diversification in many of the economies of the Global South makes them very vulnerable to the impact of the recession. On the way up some of these economies benefited from the bubbles in commodity prices, which meant that huge extra revenues were suddenly being earned. But once these bubbles burst, then the downward descent was even more rapid, and incomes and revenues were hit. Many of the countries of the Global South are vulnerable in another way, because state capacity is weak, and in some cases non-existent. Failed states, and failing states, mean there are large areas with overlapping jurisdictions and sometimes no jurisdiction at all, shadowy border lands, which are prone to wars over resources and territory, and military interventions from outside powers.

The impact of the global financial crisis will therefore affect the Global South often indirectly. It is the ripples from the much larger crisis in the heartlands that will damage these societies, and they have little capacity to avoid them or respond effectively to them. A recession is bad for the Global South because it means a decline in trade volumes, and the disappearance or reduction of some markets altogether. A second source of damage is the reduction in employment, most obviously in resource extraction if prices fall too low, but also in employment in local assembly plants and call centres producing goods and services aimed exclusively at consumers in the rich countries. A third source of possible damage is that the supply of aid might dry up as recession bites and austerity programmes involving cuts in public spending of all kinds are introduced. The small but vocal lobby in the rich democracies against aid is already using the crisis as an opportunity to urge cutting back the aid budget.

One of the structural problems of the global economy is the grossly unequal distribution of income between different countries and regions of the world, and within different countries. A similar problem existed in the 1930s. A rational reordering of the global economy would seek to redistribute income and assets to make it less unequal, or at the very least to unblock some of the obstacles, such as trading rules, which make it so hard for the poor countries to escape the poverty traps into which they have been consigned. But faced with the threat of the Global South the opposite reaction, of building the West into a secure fortress, particularly to keep out immigrants, is also likely, especially in Europe. The pressures to protect the living standards of the populations already within the rich countries will mount quickly as the recession intensifies. Every state will look to protect its own interests, and the willingness of countries to set them aside and cooperate for the greater good and in their own long-term interests will be limited. Global Keynesianism in the past required a dominant power able to play a hegemonic role and orchestrate collective solutions, which, while paying due attention to its own interests, also sought to create a wider order from which many others would benefit. The question is whether any state or group of states could play that role today.

Transfer of Hegemony

The United States was very hard hit by the way it responded to the Great Crash and by the Great Depression which followed, yet that great capitalist crisis was seen in retrospect as the decisive watershed between Britain's hegemony and the new American hegemony. What the crisis demonstrated was that the old order was bust beyond repair, and that Britain no longer had the capacity even if it had the will to do anything about it. There could not be a return to the gold standard and the financial and commercial dominance of London. Britain remained one of the leading economies in the world, and still controlled its largest empire, but its credit and its asset base was much depleted after the First World War, and its industrial productivity and industrial capacity was now well behind that of the United States. The American economy performed below its potential throughout the 1930s, but its potential was still unmistakeable. Just how great it had become was shown in the Second World War, when full mobilization of its resources created an industrial and military machine which overwhelmed Japan and helped to overwhelm Germany. By 1945 there was no doubt about the relative power of Britain and the United States. Only Russia could deploy a military power to match that of America, but was no match industrially.

What made the United States so strong in the 1930s despite the depression was the lead it had established in industry and in finance. It had become the world's largest economy and the richest economy, and was at the forefront in developing new cutting-edge technologies and new ways of organizing the economy, of building cities and of providing mass transportation and mass consumption. The United States was increasingly viewed as a new civilization, a new form of modernity which in its scale and scope and novelty was different from anything previously experienced. Britain had been revolutionary in its day too, but now had been eclipsed.

In the 1970s, in the second major capitalist crisis of the twentieth century, the continued hegemony of the United States was called into question, and in the 1980s there was a lively debate on the possibilities of US decline. It was certainly true that it had lost some of the dominance it had possessed just after the Second World War. Countries like Germany and Japan, which had been devastated by defeat and occupation, had taken time to rebuild but now were strong economically again, and in some fields were challengers again. The financial strength of the United States had declined, the dollar had had to be floated, and the military capacity of the US had been shown to have limits. But if the United States was in danger of losing its automatic position as the hegemon, there was no obvious challenger in sight. The Soviet Union still posed a military threat to the United States, but no-one thought it still presented a serious economic challenge. The Soviet model had appeared for a short while as though it might be a real rival to the United States, but the exposure of the huge inefficiencies of the Soviet economy and its inability to diversify or to innovate except in very narrow fields placed it at a significant disadvantage. Japan and Germany might be serious economic players again, but both were both much smaller than the United States, and were in no position to assume global leadership, and showed little inclination to try. There was some talk of the need for collective leadership, built around the G7 or some similar body, but this soon faded. Germany in particular realized that it was not in a position on its own to take the lead, and the United States was not keen on any formal sharing arrangement.

The talk in particular in the 1980s of Japan being in the fast lane, and about to overtake the United States because of its superior growth model and its growing financial strength, disappeared when the asset price bubble in the Japanese financial system which had been inflating very fast at the end of the 1980s suddenly burst, and the Japanese economy fell into a ten-year deflationary spiral of stagnant growth. In the meantime, the American economy, buoyed by the collapse of communism in Europe and victory in the Gulf War, now embarked on another long period of expansion, and appeared to be rediscovering its cutting edge and its ability to innovate, pioneering once again major new technologies, particularly in information and communications technology and biotechnology.

The crisis unfolding in 2009 will be at least as serious as the crisis of the 1970s, and therefore is likely to require as a minimum a substantial reorganization and redirection of the US economy. But many have begun to speculate that these events may come to assume a significance as great as the 1930s depression, not in the sense that the recession in the United States is likely to be as bad as the depression of the 1930s, but in the sense that leadership of the global economy may once again be at stake. The US has no rival at the moment, but just as the 1930s was the decisive period when it became clear that Britain could no longer act as the global leader, so the question is being raised as to whether this crisis will come to be seen retrospectively as marking the moment that the United States lost the ability and the will to reassert its global leadership, and continue to govern the global economy.

Such analyses may be getting ahead of themselves. The United States may be suffering a further relative decline – many of its capacities and its structural power are weaker than they were – and this makes the assertion of its leadership more difficult. But it still has important strengths, such as its demographic profile due to continued high levels of immigration and its continued dominance of science and innovation, and there still is no clear challenger to take over. The EU economy may be as large as the US economy, but it is internally divided, with some countries in the eurozone and some outside, and the ability of the EU to formulate common policies and deliver on them is still confined to a few areas, and in some of the most important, such as fiscal policy and defence, it is rudimentary. In many respects the EU is still subordinate to the United States and content to be so. The enlargement over recent years has weakened the coherence of the EU and its ability to present itself as a single actor.

The only other possible contender is China, but, as already argued, China is in no position to assume global leadership even it was willing to do so. It is true that, like the United States in the 1920s and 1930s, China has huge potential, which is only just being realized. If it is successful in continuing its industrialization and urbanization then at a certain stage it will become the world's largest economy. It is already one of the world's leading financial powers. It has a vast territory and a vast population, and it thinks of itself as a universal civilization. But it is at a much earlier stage of development than the United States was in 1920, and it faces huge internal problems, which arise from trying to manage such a rapid industrial transition. Its political institutions and the institutions of its civil society are much less developed than those in Europe or the United States, and this means that it does not yet possess the capacity for innovation, technological, organizational and cultural, which has been such a feature of the success of both the United States and before it of Britain.

This suggests that while China might be a contender for global leadership at some point in the future, it is not imminent. What it does mean is that China and the other emerging economies have become significant players and can no longer be ignored, so that if the United States is still to govern the global economy it will have to find some way of incorporating them. If it chooses not to there will be fragmentation and stalemate. That does not mean a return to militarized regional blocs and a drift to war. But it could mean a series of failures to secure agreements on how to tackle the problems of the global economy. The failure of the Doha Round of the WTO in 2008 might be replicated in other areas, as more and more countries seek to protect themselves as best they can and stall on wider agreements. The United States may yet emerge from this crisis as it did from the last two, still dominant, and able to project both its power and assert its leadership. But it will never be as strong again as it once was, and its leadership will have to take different forms and explore new directions. It will certainly have to adopt a new style. That will require a political class able to recognize and adjust to the reality of relative American decline, and take the appropriate steps. Winston Churchill once said that the Americans could be relied on to do the right thing, once they had exhausted all other alternatives. They may not be quite there yet.

6
What is to be Done?

As the crisis has gathered force, it has produced a flood of explanation and prescription. As always with such events there have been attempts to understand what is going on with reference to what has happened in the past. The narratives that are constructed to make sense of what is taking place seek to relate it to what is known and familiar. The past is ransacked by the media to explain the present. The twenty-four-hour news cycle has intensified this process, so that events are instantly framed and located in terms of earlier narratives to give them meaning and allow them to be understood. Each account gets endlessly repeated and recycled, every angle instantly explored, every explanation both accepted and discounted. In the midst of battles, soldiers encounter the fog of war, but there is a more general phenomenon in politics, the fog of events, which makes it hard to grasp the significance of what is taking place, to distinguish the really important from the merely ephemeral, so overloaded are the airwaves with every possible interpretation.

Events as complex and far-reaching as the global financial crash of 2008 and the recession of 2009 are bound to be surrounded by confusion and uncertainty. Much of the ground we are entering is uncharted, so that guides from the past, although essential and unavoidable, are also partial. We simply do not know what is going to happen, or how deep or critical the recession might be, or how long-lasting the effects of the global financial crash will be. Everyone makes a judgement on very incomplete information, but it is these judgements all taken together that then become part of the events and shape their outcomes. Capitalist crises are not events of nature, like earthquakes, although they sometimes induce the same sense of shock and awe. They are events created by human societies themselves, and therefore potentially controllable and avoidable. It is that knowledge which inspires debate and controversy, because everyone knows there is a lot at stake. It matters which explanation of the crisis becomes dominant, because that will shape the political response. Interpretations of the crisis become part of the politics of the crisis.

All crises are necessarily crises of ideas, of different judgements, different hypotheses, different assumptions. Amid the welter of information individuals make sense of it as best they can. They seek as much certainty as possible, and make their choices accordingly, on the basis of what they trust most and have found most reliable in the past. Casting away everything we have ever learned or thought is never easy and seldom attempted, but at certain moments it becomes necessary, because the situation is genuinely unprecedented. If there were reliable precedents we would know what to do. It is when we start to doubt that there are any reliable precedents that the magnitude of the crisis suddenly dawns on us. In *The Hitch Hiker's Guide to the Galaxy* this is the moment when the DON'T PANIC sign starts flashing.

Crises provide extraordinary opportunities for political leaders and also pitfalls. In seizing these opportunities they make or break their careers. Good judgement comes into it, but whether a judgement is good or bad is usually determined retrospectively, depending on the outcome. We have become obsessed with outcomes, and with what is called success. A different standard of judgement is more concerned with whether a judgement conforms to a principle, independently established. The outcome is irrelevant. Few politicians in the modern world, however, can afford not to be concerned with outcomes. The good politician is the successful politician, and the successful politician is the one that survives. Just occasionally politicians choose to do what they consider the right thing, rather than the expedient thing. They risk vilification or mockery as a result, and have no certainty that one day their judgement will be vindicated.

One of the complications is that there are always many different kinds of ideas in play. Ideas are sometimes thought of as general concepts which float free and unanchored above ordinary life, and remain remote from it. But there are many different kinds of ideas. All practical life involves ideas, and the opposition that is often supposed to exist between ideas and interests is an unreal opposition because the interests which individuals pursue have to be articulated as ideas before they can be pursued as interests. Knowledge in any society is dispersed and fragmented, which means that very different ideas will appear persuasive in different contexts and to different individuals.

This concluding chapter discusses some of the main ways that are already present in public discussion across the world for explaining the crisis of 2008. There is naturally a lot of variation between them and they are not self-contained. I identify five main groups – the market fundamentalists, the national protectionists, the regulatory liberals, the cosmopolitan liberals and the anti-capitalists. They overlap, and arguments from more than one are often combined. What is true of all of the arguments I have chosen is that they are rooted in political economy, and their prescriptions give a more or less prominent role to the state. Political economy is often thought to rest on the proposition that economics drives politics, and there is a sense in which that is true and remains true. But it is also committed to the proposition that in certain circumstances politics drives economics. The establishment of the conditions under which economics drives politics can only be done through politics. Like the two previous major crises of the last two hundred years this crisis will also be resolved ultimately through politics, and one of the main aspects is the battle over how the crisis is to be understood, because that determines what can be done, and what should be done, and who has the legitimacy to do it.

The Market Fundamentalists

Market fundamentalists put the priority on maintaining financial stability and safeguarding the market order, but they frequently disagree among themselves as to how best to achieve this. They are the group most obviously discomfited by this crisis. They had placed their faith in the financial growth model, and had been enthusiastic about the dominance of markets over states which globalization made possible. Some have been dismayed by the turn of events, including some Republican members of the House of Representatives in the United States. But many others are unabashed and are already seeking to lay the blame for the financial crash on regulators and governments, and to resist arguments that anything that has happened requires a major rethinking of core neo-liberal beliefs about how the economy works.

Market fundamentalists are not all alike, and it is important to distinguish between them. One of the divisions lies between neo-liberals and neo-conservatives and concerns the role of the state, the neo-conservatives being much less bothered with using the state extensively if the situation warrants. In the 1930s slump it really was the case, as discussed in Chapter 4, that the conventional wisdom was to do nothing, in the belief that doing something was likely to make things worse. The high priest of non-interventionism was Herbert Hoover who had the misfortune to preside over what became the most catastrophic period in US economic history, from 1929 to 1932. J.K. Galbraith lampooned him as the president who had perfected the 'no business' meeting, the holding of very high-profile meetings with very high-profile people, from which no action of any consequence resulted. It is not unknown today.

Hoover was not as inactive or as ineffective as he has been made out to be, but then the dominant political narrative of the Great Crash and the Great Depression came to be that of the Keynesians and New Dealers like Galbraith. The New Deal interpretation of what happened in the 1930s helped shape US politics for three decades and is still influential today. The New Dealers turned the American response to the Great Crash into a morality tale, just as the neo-liberals managed to do with the American response to the 1970s stagflation. For the New Dealers the US Government, by adhering to fixed unchanging rules in 1930, failed to understand the seriousness of the situation and as a result made it very much worse by the actions that were taken. Later neo-liberal economists like Milton Friedman rejected the New Deal and Keynesian remedies for the depression, but still found fault with the inaction of the financial authorities. By reacting passively to the slump they managed to do the exact opposite of what they should have done. They drastically reduced liquidity in the system at a time when, according to Friedman, they should have been substantially increasing it. If they had done so, he argued, the Great Depression would have been avoided. The obvious corollary was that no Great Depression need ever happen again. Economists know too much.

Yet the reason why the Federal Reserve and all the other Central Banks contracted the money supply in the wake of the Great Crash was that they believed this was the right thing to do, both on grounds of basic principles of political economy, and because it was thought the surest way to stabilize the economy and make the downturn as short as possible. The idea of operating counter-cyclically was thought to be fraught with risk, liable to corrupt the business classes and load the state with debt. Advocating doing nothing was a more positive policy than it implied. It meant allowing the crisis to take its course, it meant purging the system of all the toxic debt and poor decisions and uncompetitive firms that had built up in the years of boom. The market fundamentalists then and now argue that this is healthy and perfectly normal for a capitalist economy. Without periodic bouts of destroying old values, the economy cannot recover. Green shoots of recovery can only emerge after much of the existing vegetation has been burned to the ground.

Hayek maintained this position against Keynes in the 1930s. He believed that the first priority was to balance the budget, irrespective of the effects on bankruptcies and unemployment. This was not because Hayek was especially callous or unaware of the impact of the slump on so many people. It was just that his theory and his experience in Austria told him that the downturn would only last a short time, perhaps as little as six months, provided governments had the political courage to make it sharp enough and deep enough. Only if sufficient existing value was wiped out could a quick recovery be expected. If the downturn was only partial, and particularly if the government and the financial authorities intervened to cushion its effects by protecting firms and jobs, there would be a risk of perpetuating the downward spiral and entering a long period of stagnation.

In political terms Hayek was at one with the orthodox central bankers of the time and the financial establishment, who also believed that the priority in the crisis should be the restoration of sound money. A capitalist economy could not function properly unless there was confidence in the currency as a unit of exchange and a store of value. The most important task of the state was to make sure that this was so. If money was sound then enterprise would soon revive. Any difficulties would be temporary. Individuals with money capital would soon return to the market and start increasing employment once more. To do otherwise would be to risk moral hazard, by changing the information and the incentives available to individuals in markets. Adam Smith had pointed to the risks of corruption if the business classes were not disciplined by competition, and an essential part of the discipline of competition was the discipline which sound money imposed. Businesses which got into debt and were no longer considered credit-worthy would go bankrupt. The cost of misjudging the market and making the wrong decisions was business failure. This kept the market moral, or as moral as it could ever be.

The other strand of this argument, which was particularly prominent in the 1970s stagflation, was the incompetence of government and of regulation. Government was essential but only for very limited and defined purposes, such as sound money, and even this had come to be doubted by Hayek and others by the 1970s. It became one of the hallmarks of the neo-liberal persuasion not just that that government is best which governs least, but that market solutions are always to be preferred to government solutions. The incompetence of government bureaucracies was built on a critique of four decades of increasing government intervention in economic and social life. The strength of this view was on show in the arguments of members of the House of Representatives, rejecting the bank bailout announced by Treasury Secretary Hank Paulson in September

2008. Many conservative Republicans objected to bailouts in principle. If the banks had made mistakes they should pay for them. Bailouts were an unacceptable extension of state control and intervention in the private sector. Once the government owned and directed a large part of the financial sector, it would be hard for it to relinquish these powers. The sight of the former Chairman of Goldman Sachs announcing the nationalization of the banks signalled capitulation. For many Republicans this was nothing but socialism. What they thought had been buried once and for all when the Soviet Union collapsed was making a comeback in the heartland of capitalism.

The same arguments were put against the fiscal stimulus plan which Obama and Tim Geithner put through Congress. Two hundred American economists signed an advertisement in national papers saying that more government spending would not improve economic performance, and disputing that public spending in the New Deal had worked, and many Republican Senators and Representatives argued that it was simply wrong to increase the burden of public debt, particularly on future generations, and to distribute funds according to the spending priorities of Democrats in Congress. They were setting down markers against a President determined to push ahead with state action to promote an economic recovery.

For market fundamentalists the course of the financial crash and the attitudes that have formed about it have been deeply disturbing to some of their core beliefs, because of the charge that one of the main causes of both the bubbles and the crash were the free market policies and the deregulation promoted so successfully as the new American growth model from the 1980s onwards. A strong rearguard defence has been mounted against this, developing the argument that the problem was caused not by too little but too much regulation. If deregulation had been allowed to go further then the market itself would have sorted out the problems. In particular the blame has been pointed at central banks which intervened to hold down interest rates, as the Fed did between 2000 and 2006, causing, it is suggested, a big inflation of the housing bubble. Credit was too cheap, and bad banking practices drove out the good. Bankers, to survive, had to compete in offering cheaper credit. An explosion of lending and consumption took place which a policy aimed at maintaining sound money would have cut short.

The radical position among the market fundamentalists is to question the future of central banks. It strays into anarcho-capitalist territory and follows Hayek's lead in a pamphlet he wrote in the 1970s. He argued there that the best way to ensure sound money is not through the classical liberal mechanism of a strong central bank with powers as the lender of last resort and a currency anchored to an immutable standard of value such as gold, but by allowing all currencies to be accepted as legal tender within each national jurisdiction and allowing them to compete against one another. In this way the sound currencies would drive out the unsound. Such a radical solution would mean that central banks would no longer have exclusive control over the money supply, and would therefore no longer distort the market by their actions, whether attempting to manage demand or to hit a particular inflation target. Instead, currencies would succeed or fail, depending on how they were judged by the market and whether individuals wished to hold them.

This is a fringe position, although powerfully argued by adherents of the free banking school, such as Kevin Dowd and Murray Rothbard. There is little prospect, however, of any government responding to the present crisis by abolishing its central bank. The primary concern of governments during the financial crisis has been how to stop the banking system collapsing. The financial authorities in the economies hardest hit by the crash have been using every possible measure to prevent deflation and preserve some financial stability. Many different schemes – fiscal stimulus, bank recapitalization, bank nationalization, slashing of interest rates, quantitative easing – are being tried to see what if anything will work. In a crisis such as this many market fundamentalists abandon their faith in the market and support intervention, and strong intervention by the state. There are only a few who continue to object on principle to all government intervention in the markets. For the moment the neo-liberal persuasion, which has carried all before it for so long, is on the defensive. The banking system which was once so lauded has failed catastrophically, and now has to be painfully rebuilt.

Another strand of market fundamentalism, however, does not feel defensive. Neo-conservatives have a much surer grasp of politics, and a much more pragmatic attitude to policy. Unlike many neo-liberals, they have no qualms about using the state. Neo-conservatives draw a great deal from Austrian economics and championed the supply-side policies of the Reagan era. Typical representatives of this view are Irwin Stelzer, Dominic Lawson and Amity Shlaes. For Shlaes the priority in this crisis is not sound money but encouraging enterprise. The way to do this is through deep tax cuts, preferably for companies. The aim is to make companies more profitable, which will make it more likely that they will start expanding employment rather than cutting it. If this means borrowing a great deal more, that is acceptable in the short run. Their market fundamentalism is revealed in their opposition to further regulation. The crisis, they think, should not be used as an excuse to re-regulate the economy, and impose lots of new restrictions. Regulation will cramp enterprise. Similarly, taxing the rich or trying to redistribute wealth will dry up the sources of it. Capitalists can get the economy moving again but only if they are given their head, which means slashing their taxes, and slashing the taxes of ordinary citizens so that they start spending more.

This version of market fundamentalism owes much to Joseph Schumpeter. It accepts that capitalism is messy, chaotic, but also that it is dynamic and creative, so that the task in a crisis is for the state to avoid imposing controls that damage the ability of capitalists to revive the economy. Instead, the state should concentrate on ensuring that the process of creative destruction is allowed to proceed, that the obstacles in the path of recovery are removed, and that the individuals who will develop the new industries and the new products and find applications for the new technologies which will define the next upswing are given their opportunity and are encouraged by every means at governments' disposal. This kind of market fundamentalism treats the crisis as something to be managed not deplored. The crash and the recession have to be accepted as an integral part of how capitalism renews itself, and therefore what is needed are political leaders who can respond to the challenge. The strong will come through it and survive. The weak may perish but that will be to the advantage of the economy and the society in the long run. For many neo-conservatives the 1980s remains an example of how governments should run the economy, with boldness and realism, understanding what makes capitalism work, and adapting policy pragmatically to ensure that capitalists are given their head. Redistribution can wait for better times. What matters during a crisis is reconstructing the basis for renewed capitalist prosperity.

All these market fundamentalist arguments are alive and well. The blogosphere was full of them in 2008 and 2009. They were not being used much by politicians, but that may prove temporary. Politicians are concentrating on intervention to stave off collapse, and all the blame is being aimed at the hubris of bankers. But once financial stability has been restored, and the main problem is coping with the recession, the situation is much more open. Which narrative will come to predominate is not yet determined, and the market fundamentalists will bide their time, convinced that economic realities will make their arguments the dominant ones again.

In the United States their eyes are fixed on the next congressional elections and the next presidential election. They are waiting to see if Obama can deliver. If he fails or stumbles, they hope for a Republican tide in 2012.

National Protectionists

National protectionists employ very different arguments. For them the priority is the security and welfare of the national community. Protecting these is the chief responsibility of government, because they are embedded deeply in the expectations of the citizens. In times of crisis citizens look to their governments for protection, and if they do not receive it they may look elsewhere. 'Que se vayan todos' ('All of them must go') was the demonstrators' chant in the street protests in Argentina against the government during the economic collapse of 2001. Governments come under great pressure to provide that protection, and once they have provided it for one group, everyone demands it. Jobs, bank deposits, mortgages and pensions have all been highlighted in this present crisis as requiring government help. If government can bail out banks it can bail out other sectors of the economy. From a market fundamentalist standpoint the twentieth century was a disaster for economic liberalism because the belief was instilled that individuals should look for their security and their welfare to the state. Neo-liberals have been trying to root it out in recent decades in those societies where they have gained the upper hand, but they had much more to do, and now the financial crisis and the global recession threaten to reverse many of the gains that were made, as many countries lurch into another bout of intervention,

As was explored in Chapter 4, national protectionists have a range of arguments with deep appeal in a major downturn. They offer immediate, practical help, and certainly propose to do something. They put forward a myriad of schemes and proposals, to safeguard the interests and livelihood of all those groups that are threatened. They know how to respond to the popular mood, and how to play on the emotions of fear, anxiety and panic. Their basic message is one of reassurance, that the people can place their trust in leaders who will act to protect the people and shield them from the worst effects of the downturn. They will provide the basic services and the basic minimum on which the people rely.

National protectionists speak with very different ideological inflections. The socialist and social democratic movements always had a strong vein of national protectionism, which once was delivered through forms of voluntary association such as cooperatives and building societies, and later came to be delivered more through universal state welfare programmes. The five giants which the 1942 Beveridge Report in Britain promised to slay were Want, Disease, Ignorance, Squalor and Idleness. Slaying them meant putting in place the kind of permanent collective security that capitalist welfare states all instituted by degrees after 1945. Getting rid of these collective entitlements in the neo-liberal era, or even watering them down, has been far from easy, despite many attempts to do so in many different countries. Getting political agreement to move to more insurance-based systems of welfare proved very hard, even during boom years. In a deep recession the political opposition to major changes in benefits will be even stronger, and for many governments preserving the benefits will take precedence over sound money. Governments would rather borrow and risk inflation than attempt deep cuts in their welfare states.

National protectionists are strong on the right as well as the left, particularly around demands such as tighter immigration control. Increasing levels of immigration into all the rich capitalist states became a major political issue during the boom, but risks exploding in the slump. The argument for permitting immigration, particularly in those countries with declining or static birth rates, had a strong economic rationale and was supported by many economic liberals, because it was a way to bring in necessary skills, create faster economic growth, and counter trends towards an ageing population. All the rich countries came to rely on a plentiful supply of economic migrants to boost their economic growth, but it was always at the cost of frictions and tensions with the host community, over jobs, housing and cultures. Handling these in a severe economic downturn will not be easy, especially when some newspapers and some politicians will seek to highlight them. Although the downturn itself may cause a sharp reduction in economic migration, it will not remove it altogether, and there are already many immigrants in the advanced economies, either legally or illegally, living in settled communities, many of whom have acquired citizenship. The rhetoric of the radical right and tabloid newspapers does not make fine distinctions, however, and if national protectionism takes hold during the recession minority communities will be scapegoated.

There are many national protectionists on both right and left, however, who have nothing to do with anti-immigrant politics, but who nevertheless argue that a closing of the border to new immigrants is essential in the downturn to reassure the host community that the priority of the government is to maintain their security. Frank Field, a former Labour minister, has made this argument in the UK. Tightening of border controls seems almost inevitable in this downturn, and indeed it has already started. Politicians promise jobs for their own workers, but find it hard to deliver without breaking international agreements. Many national protectionists want to go further, and propose controls on the movements of goods and capital as well as the movement of people. Tariffs and capital controls are blunt but effective means by which a state can try and limit competition and prevent capital shifting abroad. Such measures, however, if pushed too far threaten the incorporation of a national economy into the global economy, and so dependent on overseas trade have national economies become that it is a viable strategy only for a few less developed or very large states. For most of the rest, national protectionism can only be indulged in selectively and partially.

The argument of national protectionists has always been powerful for developing and rising economies, and it tends to become more powerful in downturns. If the global recession lasts a long time then there will inevitably be some turning away from the global economy and an attempt to seek economic security within relatively closed borders. Once a protectionist cycle begins it is hard to stop. The imposition of controls is highly visible, the longer-term consequences of imposing them much less so. Nationalism generally wins in these situations, and the ability of liberals to prevent it will be sorely tested if the recession lasts any length of time. In the 1930s Keynes came to advocate protectionism as a necessary step, as did Roosevelt. In the 1970s there was strong support for protectionism, particularly on the left. Protectionism is not the cause of the slump or the recession, but it can prolong it and it can make a full recovery more difficult.

National protectionists also give strong support to counter-cyclical policies and the kind of automatic stabilizers such as unemployment pay which Keynesians promoted in order to damp down economic fluctuations and prevent such violent swings in economic activity which characterized the old capitalist business cycle. A major downturn reinforces political support for those stabilizers, and for the extension of state control into new areas. Once the security narrative takes hold it is hard for governments to fail to respond to it, because if they appear to ignore it the claims will be taken up by their political rivals. Scapegoating minorities is one thing but attacking or appearing to avoid issues which touch the economic security of the majority is perilous. Politicians do not find it easy to stand on a platform of tax increases and public spending cuts during a recession. They are more likely to offer tax cuts and to promise to maintain core public spending, as well as giving many new guarantees to particular groups about their entitlements and the support they can expect from government. Governments around Europe were very reluctant to match the Irish Government's undertaking in 2008 to protect all bank deposits against default, since this seemed to remove entirely any accountability of the banks for their behaviour. But, if it came to it, no government could stand by and allow the collapse of one of the mainstream commercial banks and the wiping out of the savings of millions of depositors. In September 2008 the authorities in the United States allowed Lehman Brothers to fold, mainly it seems because it was an investment bank rather than a retail bank, and therefore did not have many millions of depositors. But the reactions to that decision almost pushed the global financial system into meltdown. How much more serious would be the refusal to protect the deposits in a major commercial bank? The nationalizations and partial nationalizations of the banking system that took place in many countries in 2008 and continued in 2009 were a classic national protectionist policy. Whatever might be the superior logic of the market fundamentalist case, the political risks of following it in a major downturn are never going to make it very appealing to governments.

In the short run national protectionist arguments are irresistible, and governments do not generally resist them. The issue then becomes how far to press them. Some national protectionists argue for sweeping controls to be extended to trade, capital and labour. The logic is impeccable and each step begets the next. Very quickly an economy can become much more closed. It provides some reassurance to the citizens and reduces their insecurity, but it also implies the acceptance in the long run of lower living standards and austerity. Such a stance can be popular for a while, but it is the surest route to stagnation, and rising tensions between states. Almost all political leaders declare themselves against national protectionism, and declare themselves against repeating the mistakes of the 1930s, but since all states have different interests, the difficulties in getting agreements to maintain openness are large, and the incentives for protecting national citizens by discrete measures strong. As already noted, the US Congress in January and February 2009 inserted 'Buy American' clauses into the major stimulus package before it, which the Administration had then to try to remove. It could be a foretaste of things to come. If general protectionism takes hold in the advanced economies, it will mean a much lower level of activity in the global economy than before 2007 and for a long time.

Regulatory Liberals

Regulatory liberals occupy a middle position. Their priority in the present downturn is the preservation of a relatively open global economy. The consequences of a major contraction of world trade, the closure of national economies and the formation of regional blocs are considered disasters which should be avoided at all costs. The failure to avoid it in the 1930s and the success in avoiding it in the 1970s are cited as two important precedents from which contemporary governments must learn.

The lessons of the 2008 crisis, as regulatory liberals see it, are twofold. The excesses of neo-liberalism have to be curbed and a new regulatory structure has to be set in place. Grave policy errors and intellectual errors accompanied the upswing, and the crash is an opportunity to take stock and correct them. The fundamentals of the system, however, in this perspective, do not need changing. An open liberal trading and investment order, private property and the rule of law remain its essential building blocks. What need to be considered are specific reforms to the international financial architecture, and a new domestic regulatory regime. The latter will not be the same in all countries, because some countries became much more exposed in the financial markets during the upswing than others. Regulatory authorities behaved differently in different parts of the world, so some do not need to consider major changes. Those countries like Iceland, Ireland and the UK, which encouraged their financial sectors to expand much faster than the rest of the economy, have the most major adjustments to make. But all countries will be forced to consider some tightening of regulation on the banks and financial services, so huge are the losses, and so irresponsible and reckless so much of the behaviour now appears. When a single bank (the Royal Bank of Scotland) can announce an annual loss of £20 billion with accounting losses running to £47 billion, it is not hard to see the force behind the demands for new regulation that will prevent that ever happening again, since the consequences for the rest of the economy are so serious.

There has been, for a long time, debate around proposals for a new financial architecture, pinpointing the inadequacies of the present regulatory structure, and these have been regularly renewed whenever there was a new financial crisis, such as the East Asian crisis of 1997. But because these crises were contained and did not spread, the progress in agreeing regulatory reform was slow. Market fundamentalists argued, generally successfully, that there was no need for such reform, and that additional regulation would place fresh burdens on enterprise and slow down the growth of the global economy. They welcomed the East Asian crisis as marking the death throes of the East Asian model of capitalism, and believed it would force East Asia to adopt the open, flexible deregulated financial markets of the Anglosphere. Elaborate economic theories were devised purporting to show that the increased sophistication of the financial markets made the financial system fundamentally stable. There would be occasional bubbles and occasional crises, but these could be isolated without damaging the whole. As the ancient proverb put it: 'Those whom the gods wish to destroy they first make mad.'

There were always, through the years of the bubble economy, voices warning about potential catastrophe. There were a number of financial newsletters which regularly predicted meltdown and advised their subscribers what to do with their assets to avoid the coming crash. When bubbles did arise and then burst, as in East Asia and as with the dot.com bubble in 2000, the doomsayers confidently proclaimed that this was the time, this was the reckoning; they proved no more correct in their timing than those predicting the end of the world. But they did get the big picture right. There was something profoundly unstable about the global economy which was built up in the bubble years, which a number of people did see very clearly. There were even some novels written around plots that assumed a gigantic financial crash. The longer the boom went on, however, the more it seemed such fears were groundless.

Much more authoritative than the financial newsletters were the small band of economists and political economists who were not swept away by the passion for efficient markets or blinded by the superior wisdom of high finance or swayed by the utopian visions of the market fundamentalists. From the 1980s there was a steady stream of pointed criticism of the risks that were being run by the deregulation of the financial markets. These critics did not all agree, but they generally shared a belief that the crisis of the 1970s had been resolved in a way which created the conditions for the next crisis. The foundations on which the prosperity of the post-war economy were built had been recklessly and needlessly thrown away. In its place had emerged what Susan Strange called 'casino capitalism', a capitalism in which finance had become the driver, and which involved taking huge risks with the jobs, pensions and savings of ordinary citizens. In a later book, written just before her death in 1998, Strange denounced what she called 'Mad Money' and drew attention to the huge perils which the global economy was running, discussing possible scenarios, one of which foresaw a major breakdown followed by a depression. She would have been horrified but not surprised by the events of 2008 and 2009. It corresponds to the worst-case scenario she outlined in that book, written ten years before.

The intellectual case of the liberal regulators has been gathering strength, put by high-profile figures including Joseph Stiglitz, Paul Krugman and George Soros, and many governments around the world, including the Obama Administration and the EU Commission, are now dominated by them. But although the risks that the global economy was running were pointed out on many occasions, the existing regulatory authorities did not have the confidence, until the crash arrived, to challenge the financial markets. The problem, as John Eatwell has expressed it, was that 'the regulators accepted that firms had the technical skills, expressed in mathematical risk models, to manage risk better than the regulator could' (Eatwell, 2008). The key argument of the liberal regulators is that the position has to be restored where the regulator is back in control, and finance back on the leash. Arrangements have to be put in place to separate once again ordinary retail banking from investment banking, so that the public utility side of banking, money as a means of exchange, is not endangered by speculative activity. A range of measures have been proposed, many of which are likely to be adopted in due course by the leading economies, which will reduce the size of the financial sector and the range of its activities. Sound and safe banking will be back, but that will mean that lending will be much tighter, loans much harder to come by, and repayment terms more onerous. If the capitalist system is to survive, then the programme of the liberal regulators or something close to it will have to be adopted. Allowing the economy to be driven by finance in the way that it has been for the last thirty years will not be seen again soon, perhaps not for a generation. The excesses of the bubble economy will not be repeated – that is, until the next time.

The programme of the regulatory liberals is the most practical set of remedies on offer, and it has growing support in the political class in many countries. But it faces major difficulties because it still rests on the willingness of the leading states in the global economy to make agreements which will involve some of them, and particularly the Americans, making concessions, about such things as the reserve currency status of the dollar (the Russians and Chinese are calling for a number of linked currencies to perform that role) and the rules governing trade. The 1930s and the 1970s both show that the creation of a viable international framework for the global economy is a necessary condition for a full recovery and the resumption of growth. It proved possible in those two periods because of the ability and the willingness of the United States to exercise leadership. But it took a decade in each case, during which the global economy passed through some tough times. The United States is now in a relatively weaker position, which makes success less likely. The tendency at a certain point to fall back upon national protectionism because finding international agreement is just too difficult will be strong.

Cosmopolitan Liberals

Cosmopolitan liberals envisage a world which nowhere exists, but which they think ought to exist. They share some of the same concerns as regulatory liberals with tightening regulatory control over the economy, but they go further. For them the priority is to establish new forms of global governance, to push the world towards acknowledging that it is becoming a polity, and to start organizing it as one. New forms and spaces for deliberation, decision and choice have to be established across the globe, in order to address the many challenges that exist, and to begin to find solutions for the many situations where the need for joint action between nations and groups is obvious enough, but where there are obstacles that prevent it from taking place. Cosmopolitan liberals want this situation rectified by creating new institutions and encouraging spontaneous new movements from below to make demands and put pressure on the existing regime.

The goal is a global polity, although not necessarily a global government, which is only one possible outcome of the cosmopolitan agenda. Apart from the practical difficulties of instituting a global government, there are also strong reservations among cosmopolitan liberals about the desirability of entrusting too much power to a centralized and monolithic organization. They celebrate civil society and its diversity rather than the state, and want to see power dispersed for most activities, while retaining a capacity for action by the whole global community when it is required. Finding a way to make both possible is hard enough within national polities, and would be even more difficult globally. But that is the cosmopolitan vision and their political challenge. Cosmopolitan liberals are found particularly in international agencies such as the UN, in many non-governmental organizations which campaign on such issues as human rights, famine relief and climate change, and in universities, particularly among lawyers, political scientists and philosophers concerned with issues of international law, human rights, global governance and social justice. Some of the world's leading thinkers, such as Jurgen Habermas, are cosmopolitan liberals.

The most radical aspect of the demands cosmopolitan liberals make is for putting world politics on a new basis, extending representation to all groups and all nations within the international agencies and the new institutions for global decision-making that they want to see established. This means sweeping away the G7, the club of the rich and powerful, and replacing it with at least the G20. Some would go further. The rising economic powers would have to be fully acknowledged as the global economic players they have become, and the importance of the western powers scaled back. This is not a trivial shift, since the group of rich nations has remained virtually the same for a hundred years, Japan being the only significant new entrant. There has been some rearrangement of the places on the upper deck, but no extra places created.

The purpose of such changes is to put the global economy on a new basis, and world economic growth on a new basis. Stable long-term growth can only be achieved if there is first a massive redistribution of wealth and power within the global polity. Cosmopolitan liberals are not anti-capitalists; a functioning global market economy is still essential, in order to prevent any slide into protectionism. Cosmopolitan liberals are opposed to market fundamentalists, but also to national protectionists. In that sense they are the inheritors of Cobden's vision of a world of commerce and peace, but with the added dimension that they believe the only way to secure it is through building the institutions of a cosmopolitan democracy which embraces the whole world. Only then would international agencies have the legitimacy to govern the global economy in the interests of everyone. What is important is that every nation should have a voice, and be given recognition.

The feasibility of building such a polity has always attracted scepticism from realists, nationalists, market fundamentalists and conservatives, among others. But cosmopolitans are on the rise, partly because the more a global economy has developed, the greater the contrast appears between a (relatively) unified global economy and a fragmented international state system. The global financial crisis exposes the political fragility of the order that has been constructed, and the great dangers the world runs if it cannot be repaired and reshaped. There is a much greater likelihood of the order disintegrating than of it being reformed, because the interests

upholding the old regime remain so strong. Even changing the membership of bodies like the IMF and the World Bank to reflect the new realities
in the global economy, or changing the membership of the UN Security
Council, is hard enough. To create new agencies which would have the
resources and the authority to tackle global warming and global poverty
would require much more.

For cosmopolitan liberals the financial crisis is an opportunity to make
the case for a fundamental recasting of global institutions, to make them
inclusive and representative. The difficulty is how to achieve this in a
world divided into rich and poor countries, powerful and weak states. The
disparities are so great, even within countries, that the obstacles to overcoming them appear impossibly large. But cosmopolitan liberals are
undaunted. They believe that overcoming these obstacles is vital if the
global economy is to be placed on a secure and stable basis. Otherwise this
financial crisis and this recession will one day be forgotten and the same
problems will eventually return.

One reason for the confidence of cosmopolitan liberals in the eventual
triumph of their ideas, despite the evidence which suggests the contrary, is
that they believe soft power can supplant hard power in the modern world.
The Cobdenites argued that the more that societies engaged with one
another in trade the less likely they would be to fight. Economic interdependence came to be seen as a condition for the perpetual peace envisioned
by Immanuel Kant, but cosmopolitan liberals have argued that it was not
enough. The existence of representative institutions, the rule of law and
republican constitutional states were also necessary. In this way
cosmopolitan liberals imagine a rational reconstruction of the world order.
In looking for models, the United Nations is less relevant to this vision
than the EU. The UN has managed to be inclusive by basing itself on the
principle of national self-determination, but that means it has had to accept
as members many authoritarian and despotic regimes, and this has
hampered the development of a common will and the application of
common principles of law and human rights across the world. The EU is
closer to what is envisaged. It is limited because its members are mainly
rich countries, but it has become an influential alternative model of international association by functioning largely as a civilian power rather than
as a military power or as a great power. As a league of democratic and
constitutional states, it is an example of soft power in operation, obliging
all those applying for membership to meet certain thresholds in respect of
human rights and democratic principles. The question mark over the EU is

how far its special character is only possible because it has grown up within the American security umbrella. Its critics suggest that without that security umbrella the EU model could not survive in its present form. Even if it can, the EU model has many flaws, the disconnect between European elites and citizens being one of the most deep-rooted, and it is not easy in any case to conceive how this kind of association might be extended to the international community as a whole, and overcome the present division into rich, poor and emerging nations.

The cosmopolitan liberal vision is an attractive one but its lack of realism is a fatal drawback. Reconstructing the governance of the global economy by making it much more inclusive could bring permanent deadlock. The EU is hardly a model of decisive, effective government. What the world may need is not a G8 or a G20 but a G2, an understanding between the United States and China, and, difficult though that will be to secure, it might in the end contribute more to the maintenance of an open world economy.

Anti-capitalists

When there is a full-blown capitalist crisis the time for the gravediggers has arrived. But their ranks have been depleted in the last three decades as socialism, the main twentieth-century alternative to capitalism, steadily lost both its intellectual and its practical appeal. Now it is the green movement that provides the sharpest critique. In the first half of the twentieth century, the presence of a large organized working class allied to a vigorous and vociferous socialist intelligentsia created the possibility that capitalism might one day face a final crisis. But after capitalism survived the Great Depression and the Second World War and a new liberal order was constructed under American leadership after 1945, the crises that have erupted since then, both large and small, have not really threatened the continuation of capitalism. The economic and political failure of the Soviet Union convinced many socialists that capitalism represented the horizon of the possible in modern society, and that effort should be devoted to reforming and improving it rather than replacing it.

There has remained a radical element in western politics which continues to reject capitalism as either a necessary or desirable form of social and economic organization. The main vehicle for this protest in the last twenty years has been the anti-globalization movement, which attracted attention for its protests at G8 summits, some of which produced clashes with the police. The anti-globalization movement has been successful in raising awareness of the costs and inequities of globalization, but it remains a very diverse coalition, with a range of different purposes. What unites most of its members is that they reject the label of anti-globalization, a label they acquired because of the protests that were orchestrated against the free trade policies which the Washington Consensus favoured. Most of the activists in the anti-globalization movement are internationalists, and therefore support alternative forms of globalization rather than seeking to destroy globalization and replace it with national protectionist forms of economy. There are genuine opponents of all forms of globalization but they tend not to be found in the ranks of the anti-globalization movement.

Anti-capitalists argue that the present crisis has come about, as all such crises do, through the elevation of profit over social need. The imbalances in the global economy, the inequalities and the financial bubbles have their origins in an economic model which gives incentives to accumulate for its own sake, and encourages every means available to maximize profits. Any weakness, whether in a state, a workforce, a market or a company, is ruthlessly exploited. The benefits of neo-liberal globalization accordingly accrued to a narrow elite of financiers, corporate directors and property holders. By the time of the 2008 crash the top 1 per cent of the US economy had 16 per cent of the income of the world's richest country, and the top 10 per cent had 46 per cent. The bonus culture provided, in the neo-liberal era, extraordinary opportunities for the corporate class to enrich itself, at the expense of almost everyone else on the planet.

The collapse of the neo-liberal model in 2008 is, for anti-capitalists, a rare opportunity to advance alternatives to the dominant ideas and institutions of contemporary capitalism. It creates openings in which other arguments get a hearing, and in which popular pressure can force the state to intervene in ways which do not simply shore up the existing system, but begin to replace it with something better. Most anti-capitalists acknowledge that this crisis, global though it is, will not give new life to socialism. Its most likely resolution will be a strengthened capitalism, even possibly a strengthened neo-liberalism, purged of some of the excesses of the last twenty years. But they also think that it could mark a stage in the strengthening of non-capitalist and anti-capitalist institutions at all levels of the global economy.

A key demand of anti-capitalists, therefore, is that the banks should be nationalized and should stay nationalized. This is partly based on the observation that countries like India, where the banks were already nationalized, did not get drawn into the financial imbroglio in the same way. The main point, however, is that only if the state takes control and keeps control of the financial sector can the economy be reoriented to social need. The financial growth model which underpinned the recovery from the 1970s stagflation depended on giving maximum freedom to finance to drive the pursuit of profit in all sectors of the economy. The rise of private equity, the hedge funds and the investment banks was based on developing techniques to extract the maximum possible surplus from existing businesses, stripping out their assets, shrinking their workforces and forcing those that remained to accept worse pay and conditions, increasing their debt ratios. In the process, anti-capitalists argue, the real purpose of the economy and of economic activity got lost, and the economic security of millions of workers throughout the global economy deteriorated. If the banks were controlled by the state then investment and lending could be directed to creating long-term jobs, and long-term security. The state, in alliance with the pension funds and other major institutional investors, as Robin Blackburn has argued, could establish a different set of priorities for the conduct of the economy, such as promoting employee rights, sustainable production methods and appropriate levels of executive compensation. He points to the Norwegian state social fund, and pension funds like Californian Public Employees Retirement System (CalPERS) as possible models.

Such a strategy could also allow many different kinds of organization to come into existence and to survive, in particular the development of not-for-profit companies, such as mutuals and trusts, forms of company organization that were not dependent on the need to maximize shareholder value. The mutual building societies in Britain which had been originally a product of working-class communities, owned by their members like the cooperative societies and dedicated to social purposes, and providing a safe form of saving and a reliable means of providing credit for home loans, were demutualized in the 1990s, and transformed into profit-making banks, to take advantage of the credit boom. Many of them collapsed in the financial crash of 2008. A means to preserve a wider organizational ecology and a means of subordinating shareholder value to wider stakeholder value are key objectives, not confined to anti-capitalists.

The anti-capitalist strategy for dealing with the financial crisis is therefore not to call for the expropriation of the expropriators but to demand that the state intervenes to create new countervailing institutions to overcome the domination of the banks and the large multinationals, which between them are regarded as responsible for the current downturn. These counter-vailing institutions with state support might in time begin to develop a new economy which gives a much higher priority to social need than commercial profit. Such an economy, for most anti-capitalists, would also have to be a green economy, because of the threat posed by climate change and environmental destruction. Part of the green movement is not just anti-capitalist but also opposed to all forms of globalization, seeking to recreate small-scale, self-sufficient economies, applying Ghandian principles. But many greens accept that there is no way back to a simpler lifestyle and a pre-industrial world, and advocate instead, like socialist anti-capitalists, an alternative form of globalization, one which would promote sustainability for the planet, and establish the institutions and the agencies necessary to do that, and promote the adoption of green technologies.

The implications for the global economy are immense, since these changes would require a gradual but persistent redistribution of wealth and power within national societies and within the global economy, and the use of state power at both national and global level to fashion a very different kind of economy and society, in which types of organization, the nature of work and individual lifestyles would all be transformed. Such a major change in direction would encounter stiff resistance, and would be very hard indeed to accomplish, especially given the weakness of the forces which anti-capitalists can call on. The obstacles are formidable, but overcoming them is not impossible. The New Deal programme in the United States in the 1930s also encountered very serious opposition, but it did succeed in setting a different direction for American capitalism which was sustained in part until the 1970s. It was not anti-capitalist, but it offended a large number of capitalist interests. A serious green programme would also offend established capitalist interests and would be strongly opposed. Its effects on lifestyles would also generate a great deal of popular opposition which might be mobilized against it, so it would require leadership skills of a high order to carry through. But like the New Deal it is the kind of programme which might effect the changes capitalism actually needs in order to survive. Capitalism needs not just a financial reconfiguration but also a political and ideological reconfiguration, and the changes need to be global. It is a paradox of capitalism as a system that often its best friends have been not its strongest supporters but its enemies. Radical pressure to transform capitalism has sometimes had unintended consequences which have given it a further lease of life.

Many anti-capitalist intellectuals live in the metropolitan West, and have their roots in the once powerful socialist movements that were based there. But the forces of change tend to lie outside the metropolitan centres, among the rising economic powers and the countries of the Global South. The ideological and political challenge was once much stronger, fuelled in particular by the anti-colonial struggle and wars of liberation. In the neo-liberal era, most of the anti-capitalist revolutionary regimes have gradually been absorbed into the global economy, and have abandoned in practice their oppositional stance, even if they maintain it in their rhetoric. The difficulty of prospering outside the global economy contributed to this, as well as the conditions attached to aid and the structural adjustment packages imposed on many developing economies by the international agencies. The implosion of the Soviet Union and the pro-market turn in China has meant that the most reliable source of anti-capitalist argument has been turned off. In recent years anti-capitalist defiance has been left to a few communist survivors, particularly Cuba and North Korea; states like Venezuela, able to take advantage of their market position as a producer of oil and pursue a populist socialism; states like Burma, which remain largely isolated from the global economy; and states like Iran, created through a popular revolution and possessing a radical Islamic ideology. Islamic culture, in some respects, is hostile to capitalism, at least as it has developed in the West, and capitalist development in the Islamic world has been somewhat hampered as a result, although most states within Islam have found an accommodation with the global economy and do not challenge it. Iran and Syria are the two main exceptions, although the character of their regimes is very different. Radical Islamism is one of the most powerful anti-capitalist and anti-western ideologies in the contemporary world, because it rejects not just capitalism but modernity in many of its forms, but it is an ideology with a more limited appeal than socialism. The financial crisis appears to radical Islamists as the kind of disorder to be expected of the capitalist West, and confirms their desire to purge their societies of all traces of western influence. But apart from recommending that the Islamic world insulates itself still further from the west, its economy and its culture, the radical Islamists have little to recommend about solutions to the crisis. They would like the Islamic world to disengage from the West and resume its own life, free from interference from the West or involvement with it.

Spectres at the Feast

This book has been mainly concerned with the spectre of capitalist crisis, which by the beginning of 2009 was beginning to look very threatening, with the IMF predicting the worst performance of the global economy for sixty years, and the recessionary wave seemingly unstoppable, with one country after another succumbing. Internal unrest began to rise markedly also as the hardship associated with the recession began to hit more and more individuals and families. The groundswell of demand for protection was beginning to force governments' hands, even while at international meetings they redoubled their calls to resist protection and maintain the open global economy. Many actions governments took to stabilize their economies could be interpreted by other countries as disadvantaging them, and invited defensive measures in response. The Russians and Chinese began complaining that the fiscal stimulus packages announced by Washington were at the rest of the world's expense because so long as the dollar was the only reserve currency, other countries were forced to buy US Treasury bonds. The prospects of holding the international community together and preventing both a deflationary spiral and a protectionist spiral did not look good at the beginning of 2009. Quite exceptional demands and hopes were being laid on the new United States Administration that somehow, against the odds, it could broker a set of deals that could hold the global economy together.

Deflationary spirals can be halted if governments act decisively enough. Even a protectionist world allows some growth. The prospect that worries world leaders is not that they face an uncontrollable collapse, but that they face a long period of stagnation. All societies that have integrated into the global economy are geared for growth, and require growth to maintain political stability. China is an obvious example, but it is far from alone. The degree of interdependence is much higher than it was in the 1930s, and it will be harder for economies to disengage without facing very painful adjustment. This suggests there may be a willingness by many nations to compromise in a bid to create conditions in which growth might resume. But the situation may have to get very much worse before that stage is reached, and the danger is that some countries may find ways to stabilize their economies which will make them unwilling to compromise. This will prolong things. The Second World War was the event which brought the stagnation of the 1930s to an end, clearing the ground in the most radical way possible. But with 55 million dead as a result of the conflict, and unspeakable suffering and destruction, it is not an episode anyone wants to repeat.

It also cannot be repeated. Nuclear weapons have seen to that. Behind the spectre of capitalist crisis looms this second spectre, a spectre that has been haunting the world now for sixty years. The human species has acquired the means to destroy itself, and this has changed the nature of war, the nature of the international state system and the nature of sovereignty. It has made war between the great powers unthinkable, but that did not prevent the two superpowers during the Cold War from thinking it and from preparing for it. It allowed an understanding to be kept between them which meant their conflict was conducted through proxies and through means short of war, but, on at least one occasion, the Cuban missile crisis in 1962, the understanding almost failed. Since the demise of the Soviet Union the risk of a nuclear exchange between great powers reduced sharply, but it has been replaced by a new danger – the failure to stop the gradual proliferation of nuclear weapons around the world. International cooperation becomes essential to limit this danger, but it is international cooperation which is put at risk by the responses to the global financial crisis and the recession. If there is now a retreat not just from globalization but also from global governance, and from the attempt to forge international agreements, then the risk of other ways being used to settle disputes grows. Fears of other countries acquiring nuclear weapons will be used to justify pre-emptive strikes, with dramatic consequences for world peace. There has long been talk of the need to banish nuclear weapons altogether and create a nuclear-free world, but there has been little movement towards that goal, and in a time of economic hardship and heightened anxieties what movement there may be is more likely to be in the other direction.

The other spectre haunting the world is climate change. The threat it poses is less immediate than nuclear weapons, but in the long run it may be just as serious, because like nuclear weapons it is a threat to the continued existence of the species. In many ways it is not a new threat; it can be seen to have arisen with the modern age itself, and the development of modern industry. It reflects the character of capitalism and the way it has disturbed all the normal rhythms of social life and plunged the world into a situation which is not controllable. John McNeill, in his environmental history of the twentieth century, *Something New Under the Sun*, describes the extraordinary character of the last two hundred years: 'The human race without intending anything of the sort has undertaken a gigantic controlled experiment on the earth' (McNeill, 2001, p. 4). The rate of population growth, the rate of economic growth, and the rate of energy consumption are without historical precedent, and all have accelerated to such a degree that cumulatively they have placed enormous and unsustainable pressure on the planet. But no-one knows how to take back control of them.

A global recession gives some temporary respite to the build-up of these pressures, but even in a recession they continue at an unsustainable level. It is just that the degree of unsustainability does not increase quite so fast for a while. What the recession does do, however, is focus attention on the excesses and the shortcomings of the period of growth that has just ended, and allows new thinking about how to move forward. There is a determination expressed by many political leaders to ensure that the next period of growth in the global economy is built on sounder environmental foundations than the last, and that the new technologies must be green technologies. This hope for a more sustainable economy, however, has to contend with the desire to get back to normal as quickly as possible, and to see incomes, living standards and jobs increasing again as soon as possible. The rising economic powers face acute challenges in making their future growth more sensitive to environmental needs, given the pressure of their vast populations seeking a better job and a better standard of living, which has been one of the main drivers of the global economy in the last twenty years. In the short run the burden of adjustment to a low-carbon world has to be borne by the rich nations, but during a recession some of the changes and sacrifices will be fiercely resented and opposed.

There are other threats to the human species apart from nuclear weapons and climate change. The point about nuclear weapons and climate change, however, is that these are not natural threats but threats created by the human species, and in very recent time. The global downturn as such does not threaten the future of the human species, but like the other two threats it is inseparable from capitalism and from modernity. This new stage in human history has transformed the conditions of life of the human species, but at the same time exposed it to quite new dangers.

The three spectres are also interlinked because solving any one of them, let alone all of them, requires the building of a wider coalition than any that has been attempted so far in human history. It requires not just skill but political imagination. Where neo-liberalism led to a distinct narrowing of possibilities, what is now needed is a considerable expansion of them. There will have to be alternatives and experiments with different ways of doing things. During the great bubble economy, there was euphoria about the ever-increasing growth and prosperity, and absorption of the rich nations in their feast of consumption. Although there was mounting concern expressed about climate change and a consensus began to form that something must be done, no-one could quite imagine what could be done that would be anywhere near enough to make any significant difference. So locked into the pattern of growth and consumption had the rich nations become, that any radical change looked politically impracticable. Why should anyone, particularly in a democracy, take action when the threat is not immediate and palpable? There are many disturbing signs of the effects of climate warming, but still a resolute band of sceptics deny the evidence, and suggest there are other explanations. Democratic populations find it hard to deny expansion of air and car travel, or to curtail the use of energy in businesses and the home. The rich countries have become so dependent on high energy consumption and on mobility that a way of life that does not depend on these things has become almost unthinkable. A few individuals escape every year to a different way of life in remote islands, but it is not an option open to more than a handful.

The great dilemma of our time is how the world could be brought to cooperate to face these challenges and begin to manage them. In shaking the foundations of the recent prosperity and the present system of governance of the globe, the financial crash and the global recession create an opportunity for some fundamental rethinking of how we order our world, and what needs to be done to get a lasting recovery. The results are bound to be mixed, since the history of human greed and folly is not about to end, and there are no doubt still many chapters to be written. But if we can avoid relapsing into market fundamentalism or the more extreme forms of national protectionism, and building pragmatically a new system of regulation, a new international framework and a new economy, there is the glimmer of a hope that some positive things may yet be done to lift some of the clouds that lower so threateningly over us, and banish the spectres that haunt us. The outcomes lie with us, with all of us on the planet, and will depend on whether our eagerness to fight and quarrel can be contained, whether the pursuit of our self-interest can be curbed or channelled in new directions, and whether durable new forms of cooperation can emerge. Other species survive by adapting to their environment. The human species has done the same. But there is a difference. Increasing parts of the human environment have been created by the activity of the human species itself, and many of them are toxic. We face the daunting task of learning from this present crisis, and trying in the future to attempt something more different than we have ever attempted before.

Guide to Further Reading

Introduction: The Road to Excess

One of the best places to start in considering the recent rise of finance to its new position of dominance in the global economy is the work of Susan Strange (1986, 1998). Other valuable analyses of this phase of the global economy include those by Herman Schwartz (2000); Robert Cox (1996); Andrew Glyn (2006); and Peter Gowan (1999). Francis Fukuyama's original formulation of the idea of a new end of history remains a reference point for this period (Fukuyama, 1989). The excesses of this strange world are well caught by Stephen Haseler (2008) and the world of credit default swaps and financial derivatives by George Soros (2008) and Charles Morris (2008). An indispensable guide to past panics, manias and crashes is provided by Charles Kindleberger (1978). Treatments of Marx's theory of capitalist crisis can be found in Paul Sweezy (1968) and Ernest Mandel (1978). Furio Cerutti has written an important book on the other spectres at the feast, the challenge posed by nuclear weapons and global warming (Cerutti, 2007).

1 From Boom to Bust

The idea of financialization, making every citizen an independent financial subject, is explored by Paul Langley (2004), and by Herman Schwartz and Len Seabrooke (2008) in a special issue of *Comparative European Politics* which focuses in particular on housing and mortgages, and brings together some of the best younger scholars researching in political economy on different forms of individual asset holding. A useful comparative study of the Reagan/Thatcher era is the study by Kenneth Hoover and Raymond Plant (1988). The character of the era as 'privatized Keynesianism' is well caught by Colin Crouch (2008), and the nature of the 'Big Bang' and financial deregulation by Michael Moran (1990). Tim Sinclair analyses the rise of the bond rating agencies (Sinclair, 2005). Paul Krugman is illuminating on this era, and among other things on the Japanese deflation (Krugman, 2008). Alan Greenspan's memoir is also worth consulting (Greenspan, 2008). The concept of the Anglosphere in its recent neo-conservative usage is presented by James Bennett (2004) and a discussion of the older idea of Anglo-America can be found in *Between Europe and America* (Gamble, 2003). For models of capitalism, see the studies by David Coates (2000), Peter Hall and David Soskice (2001), Colin Crouch (2005), Vivien Schmidt (2002) and Ben Clift and Jonathan Perraton (2004). On the credit crunch, Robert Peston, George Soros, Stephen Haseler, Charles Morris, Paul Krugman and Peter Gowan have all written illuminatingly (Peston, 2008; Soros, 2008; Haseler, 2008; Morris, 2008; Krugman, 2008; Gowan, 2009). There are also numerous blogs and other sites worth visiting, offering many different perspectives. They include those of Paul Krugman, Martin Wolf, Robert Peston, Nouriel Roubini, Ambrose Evans-Pritchard, also *The Financial Times*, whose coverage and quality of analysis is superlative, *The Wall Street Journal* and *Open Democracy*.

2 Crises of Capitalism

A good place to start would be Andrew Shonfield's classic text on modern capitalism (Shonfield, 1965), supplemented by Geoffrey Ingham's lucid analysis of capitalism (Ingham, 2008). Classic accounts of Marxist and Austrian theories of crisis, as well as the ideas of Kondratieff, are provided by Paul Sweezy, Ernest Mandel and Joseph Schumpeter (Sweezy, 1968; Mandel, 1978; Schumpeter, 1976). One of the best more recent books on capitalist crisis is by David Harvey (1982). A useful commentary on Schumpeter is provided by Richard Swedberg (1991). Karl Polanyi's masterpiece *The Great Transformation* has recently been reissued (Polanyi, 2001). Jurgen Habermas set out the idea of capitalist crisis as a legitimation crisis in the 1970s (Habermas, 1976). The analysis of political economy as a form of discourse, and therefore of crisis as socially constructed, has been developed by Mark Blyth, Colin Hay and Vivien Schmidt (Blyth, 2002; Hay, 2002; Schmidt, 2002).

The Great Crash and the Great Depression have created an enormous literature. J.K. Galbraith's book on the crash remains a classic (Galbraith, 1955). Barry Eichengreen has written the major study of the economic causes of the Great Depression (Eichengreen, 1992), and see also the analyses by Milton Friedman and Anna Schwartz (1963) and the current Fed Chairman Ben Bernanke (2000), and the counter-arguments to Friedman and Schwarz by Peter Temin (1976). See also the classic study by Heinz-Wolfgang Arndt on the economic lessons of the 1930s (Arndt, 1944). One of the most influential later interpretations of the Depression is Charles Kindelberger's study, which pinpointed the failure of international leadership as a major contributory factor (Kindleberger, 1973). For the New Deal, Tony Badger is the most authoritative guide (Badger, 1989) and see also the shorter study by Eric Rauchway (2008). On Keynes, Robert Skidelsky's three-volume biography is indispensable (Skidelsky, 1983, 1992, 2000). Among other studies, Michael Stewart's book on the age of Keynes is one of the most valuable (Stewart, 1986). Simon Clarke analyses Keynesianism and the Keynesian welfare state (Clarke, 1987). Hyman Minsky wrote an interesting book on Keynes, which also sets out his own theories about financial markets (Minsky, 2008). For Hayek's critique of Keynesianism, a good place to start is his collection of articles, *A Tiger by the Tail* (Hayek, 1972). On the limits of social science and economics in particular, Tony Lawson is a good guide (Lawson, 1996).

3 Globalization and Neo-liberalism

Michal Kalecki's famous article on the political consequences of full employment sets out the change which Keynesianism introduced and which neo-liberalism was determined to reverse (Kalecki, 1943). On neo-liberalism, one of the most comprehensive treatments is by Rachel Turner (2008). Different standpoints on neo-liberalism can be found in the books by David Harvey, Norman Barry, John Gray and Richard Robison (Harvey, 2005; Barry, 1986; Gray, 1998; Robison, 2006). The rise of neo-liberalism has been traced by Richard Cockett (1994). Paul Pierson charts the limited impact of neo-liberal policies on welfare states (Pierson, 1994). On globalization, the most influential academic transformationalist analyses are by David Held and Anthony McGrew and Jan Aart Scholte (Held and McGrew, 2003, 2007; Scholte, 2005). Sceptical viewpoints are provided by Paul Hirst and Grahame Thompson and by Justin Rosenberg (Hirst and Thompson, 1996; Rosenberg, 2005). Kenichi Ohmae provides a version of the hyper-globalist perspective which has proved so influential (Ohmae, 1995). Other valuable contributions to the debate on globalization include those by Martin Wolf (2005), and a useful overview of the various debates is provided by Mark Rupert (2005). Michael Moran analyses the regulatory state in the neo-liberal era (Moran, 2003), while the nature of the Washington Consensus and the post-Washington Consensus is evaluated in a major study of the international political economy by Anthony Payne (2005). For a case study of neo-liberalism, see Peadar Kirby on Ireland (Kirby, 2002).

4 The Politics of Recession

The best book on the interrelationship between international political economy and domestic politics in the twentieth century is by Helen Thompson (2008). For the recent era, see also Herman Schwartz and Peter Gowan (Schwartz, 2000; Gowan, 1999). Ponzi schemes are described by Charles Kindleberger, and J.K. Galbraith is unequalled on the irrational exuberance of the upswing (Kindleberger, 1978; Galbraith, 1955). Depoliticization is set out by Stephen Gill and Peter Burnham (Gill, 1998; Burnham, 2001). For the Great Depression and for Keynes and Keynesianism, see the readings for Chapter 2. For recent US politics, the *New York Review of Books* is indispensable. For Britain, Stephen Driver and Luke Martell, Richard Heffernan and Anthony Seldon are reliable guides to the progress of new Labour (Driver and Martell, 2006; Heffernan, 1999; Seldon, 2007). On the politics of right and left, see the analyses by Noberto Bobbio and Alan Noel and Jean-Philippe ThÈrien (Bobbio, 2005; Noel and ThÈrien, 2008). Donald Sassoon provides the best historical account of European social democracy (Sassoon, 1996).

5 The Global Impact

Paul Kennedy's book on the decline and fall of the great powers remains essential reading (Kennedy, 1988). On the United States, there is a very large literature, but analyses that stand out include those by John Ikenberry, Joseph Nye, Charles Kupchan, David Rapkin, Simon Bromley and Helen Thompson (Ikenberry, 2004; Nye, 2002; Kupchan, 2002; Rapkin, 2005; Bromley, 2008; Thompson, 2008). See also the new overview by Michael Cox and Doug Stokes (Cox and Stokes, 2008). On China, see especially the books by Will Hutton and Shaun Breslin (Hutton, 2007; Breslin, 2007). Robyn Meredith provides an assessment of the rise of both India and China (Meredith, 2008). For the EU there is again a vast literature. Some of the best political economy analyses include those by Magnus Ryner and Alan Cafruny, Ben Rosamond, Vivien Schmidt and, for the euro, Kenneth Dyson (Ryner and Cafruny, 2007; Rosamond, 2000; Schmidt, 2002; Dyson, 2008). For the Global South and the politics of development in relation to international political economy, Anthony Payne provides one of the best accounts (Payne, 2005). Ha-Joon Chang has analysed in a number of writings the cost of the present liberal order for developing countries (Chang, 2003). Amrita Narlikar has analysed the particular challenges facing the WTO (Narlikar, 2005). For the problems associated with a new financial architecture, see the evaluation by Ben Thirkell-White, and also Robert Wade (Thirkell-White, 2007; Wade, 2007, 2008). On the coming demise of Eurocentrism, John Hobson is the best guide (Hobson, 2004).

6 What is to be Done?

Many of the best sources for this chapter are to be found in blogs and websites, particularly of think tanks. For market fundamentalists, in addition to the sources cited in Chapter 3, the blogs of Amity Shlaes and Irwin Stelzer's book on neo-conservatism should be consulted (Stelzer, 2005), as well as the websites of the American Enterprise Institute, the Cato Institute and the Institute of Economic Affairs. The ideas of free banking are lucidly expounded by Kevin Dowd (2001). For regulatory liberals, the contributions of Joseph Stiglitz, George Soros and Paul Krugman have been particularly influential (Stiglitz, 2002; Soros, 2008; Krugman, 2008). For cosmopolitan liberals, see the contributions of, among others, David Held and Daniele Archibugi (Held, 2004; Archibugi, 2008). For anti-capitalists, see in particular Naomi Klein, Alex Callinicos and George Monbiot (Klein, 2007; Callinicos, 2003; Monbiot, 2003, 2006). Very useful too are a number of publications and websites associated with the left and the green movement, such as *Red Pepper.* Some of the most powerful critiques of current policies in finance from an anti-capitalist position have come from Robin Blackburn in his detailed proposals for pensions (Blackburn, 2004, 2006). Paul Ginsborg has argued for a new politics of everyday life (Ginsborg, 2005). Some of the deeper challenges to our future are addressed by William McNeill, John Dunn and Furio Cerutti (McNeill, 2001; Dunn, 2002; Cerutti, 2007).

Bibliography

Arndt, Heinz-Wolfgang (1944) *The Economic Lessons of the 1930s* (New York: Oxford University Press).

Archibugi, Daniele (2008) *The Global Commonwealth of Citizens: Toward Cosmopolitan Democracy* (Princeton, NJ: Princeton University Press).

Badger, Anthony (1989) *The New Deal: The Depression Years 1933–1940* (Chicago: Dee).

Barry, Norman (1986) *The New Right* (London: Croom Helm).

Bennett, James (2004) *The Anglosphere Challenge: Why the English-speaking Countries will Lead the Way in the Twenty-first Century* (New York: Roman & Littlefield).

Bernanke, Ben (2000) *Essays on the Great Depression* (Princeton, NJ: Princeton University Press).

Blackburn, Robin (2004) 'How to Rescue a Failing Pensions Regime: The British Case', *New Political Economy* 9:4, 559–80.

Blackburn, Robin (2006) *Age Shock: How Finance is Failing Us* (New York: Verso)

Blyth, Mark (2002) *Great Transformations: Economic Ideas and Institutional Change in the Twentieth Century* (New York: Cambridge University Press).

Blyth, Mark (2008) 'The Politics of Compounding Bubbles: The Global Housing Bubble in Comparative Perspective', *Comparative European Politics* 6:3, 387–406.

Bobbio, Noberto (2005) *Left and Right: The Significance of a Global Distinction* (Cambridge: Polity).

Brenner, Robert (2006) *The Economics of Global Turbulence: The Advanced Capitalist Economies from Long Boom to Long Downturn, 1945–2005* (London: Verso).

Breslin, Shaun (2007) *China and the Global Political Economy* (Basingstoke and New York: Palgrave Macmillan).

Bromley, Simon (2008) *American Power and the Prospects for International Order* (Cambridge: Polity).

Burnham, Peter (2001) 'New Labour and the Politics of Depoliticisation', *British Journal of Politics and International Relations* 3:2, 127–49.

173

Callinicos, Alex (2003) *An Anti-Capitalist Manifesto* (Cambridge: Polity).

Cerutti, Furio (2007) *Global Challenges for Leviathan: A Political Philosophy of Nuclear Weapons and Global Warming* (Lanham, MD: Lexington Books).

Chang, Ha-Joon (2003) *Globalization, Economic Development and the Role of the State* (New York: Zed Books).

Clarke, Simon (1987) *Keynesianism, Monetarism and the Crisis of the State* (Aldershot: Edward Elgar).

Clift, Ben and Jonathan Perraton (2004) *Where are National Capitalisms Now?* (Basingstoke and New York: Palgrave Macmillan).

Coates, David (2000) *Models of Capitalism* (Cambridge: Polity).

Cockett, Richard (1994) *Thinking the Unthinkable: Think-tanks and the Economic Counter-revolution 1931–1983* (London: HarperCollins).

Congressional Research Service (2008) *Foreign Holdings of Federal Debt*, March (Washington, DC).

Cox, Michael and Doug Stokes (2008) *US Foreign Policy* (Oxford: Oxford University Press).

Cox, Robert (1996) *Approaches to World Order* (Cambridge: Cambridge University Press).

Crouch, Colin (2005) 'Models of Capitalism', *New Political Economy* 10:4, 439–56.

Crouch, Colin (2008) 'What will Follow the Demise of Privatised Keynesiansim?', *Political Quarterly* 79:4, 476–87.

Dowd, Kevin (2001) *Money and the Market: Essays on Free Banking* (London: Routledge).

Driver, Stephen and Luke Martell (2006) *New Labour* (Cambridge: Polity).

Dunn, John (2002) 'The Emergence into Politics of Global Environmental Change', in Ted Munn (ed.), *Encyclopaedia of Global Environmental Change* Vol. 5, (London: John Wiley): 124–36.

Dyson, Kenneth (2008) *The Euro at 10: Europeanisation, Power and Convergence* (Oxford: Oxford University Press).

Eatwell, John (2008) '"Greater transparency" is the mantra of the ignorant', *Guardian* 19 September.

Eichengreen, Barry (1992) *Golden Fetters: The Gold Standard and the Great Depression 1919–1939* (Oxford: Oxford University Press).

Friedman, Milton and Anna Schwartz (1963) *A Monetary History of the United States 1867–1960* (Princeton, NJ: Princeton University Press).

Fukuyama, Francis (1989) 'The End of History', *The National Interest* 16, 3–18.

Galbraith, John Kenneth (1955) *The Great Crash* (London: Hamish Hamilton).

Gamble, Andrew (2003) *Between Europe and America: The Future of British Politics* (Basingstoke and New York: Palgrave Macmillan).

Gill, Stephen (1998) 'European Governance and New Constitutionalism: Economic and Monetary Union and Alternatives to Disciplinary Neoliberalism in Europe', *New Political Economy* 3:1, 5–26.

Ginsborg, Paul (2005) *The Politics of Everyday Life: Making Choices, Changing Lives* (New Haven, CT: Yale University Press).

Glyn, Andrew (2006) *Capitalism Unleashed* (Oxford: Oxford University Press).

Gowan, Peter (1999) *The Global Gamble: Washington's Faustian Bid for World Dominance* (London: Verso).

Gowan, Peter (2009) 'Crisis in the Heartland', *New Left Review* 55, 5–30.

Grant, Wyn (2002) *Economic Policy in Britain* (Basingstoke and New York: Palgrave Macmillan).

Gray, John (1998) *False Dawn* (London: Granta).

Greenspan, Alan (2008) *The Age of Turbulence* (London: Penguin).

Habermas, Jurgen (1976) *Legitimation Crisis* (London: Heinemann).

Hall, Peter and David Soskice (2001) *Varieties of Capitalism: The Institutional Foundations of Comparative Advantage* (Oxford: Oxford University Press).

Harvey, David (1982) *The Limits to Capital* (Oxford: Basil Blackwell).

Harvey, David (2005) *A Brief History of Neo-liberalism* (Oxford: Oxford University Press).

Haseler, Stephen (2008) *Meltdown: How the 'Masters of the Universe' Destroyed the West's Power and Prosperity* (London: Forum Press).

Hay, Colin (2002) *Political Analysis* (Basingstoke and New York: Palgrave Macmillan).

Hayek, F.A. (1972) *A Tiger by the Tail* (London: IEA).

Hayek, F.A. (1978) *New Studies in Philosophy, Politics, Economics and the History of Ideas* (London: Routledge).

Heffernan, Richard (1999) *New Labour and Thatcherism: Political Change in Britain* (Basingstoke and New York: Palgrave Macmillan).

Held, David (2004) *Global Covenant* (Cambridge: Polity).

Held, David and Anthony McGrew (2003) (eds) *The Global Transformations Reader* (Cambridge: Polity).

Held, David and Anthony McGrew (2007) *Globalization/Anti-Globalization* (Cambridge: Polity).

Hirst, Paul and Grahame Thompson (1996) *Globalisation in Question* (Cambridge: Polity).

Hobson, John (2004) *The Eastern Origins of Western Civilisation* (Cambridge: Cambridge University Press).

Hoover, Kenneth and Raymond Plant (1988) *Conservative Capitalism in Britain and the United States* (London: Routledge).

Hutton, Will (2007) *The Writing on the Wall: China and the West in the 21st Century* (London: Little, Brown).

Ikenberry, John (2004) 'Liberalism and Empire: Logics of Order in the American Unipolar Age', *Review of International Studies* 30, 609–30.

IMF (2009) *World Economic Report*, January (Washington, DC).

Ingham, Geoffrey (2008) *Capitalism* (Cambridge: Polity).

Kalecki, Michal (1943) 'Political Aspects of Full Employment', *Political Quarterly* 14, 322–31.

Kennedy, Paul (1988) *The Rise and Fall of the Great Powers* (London: Unwin Hyman).

Keynes, John Maynard (1973) *The General Theory of Employment, Interest and Money*, in *The Collected Writings of John Maynard Keynes*, VII (London: Macmillan).

Kindleberger, Charles (1973) *The World in Depression, 1929–1939* (London: Allen & Unwin).

Kindleberger, Charles (1978) *Manias, Panics, and Crashes* (New York: Basic Books).

Kirby, Peadar (2002) *The Celtic Tiger in Distress: Growth with Inequality in Ireland* (Basingstoke and New York: Palgrave Macmillan).

Klein, Naomi (2007) *The Shock Doctrine* (London: Penguin).

Krugman, Paul (2008) *The Return of Depression Economics* (London: Penguin).

Kupchan, Charles (2002) *The End of the American Era* (New York: Vintage).

Langley, Paul (2004) 'In the Eye of the Perfect Storm: The Final Salary Pensions Crisis and Financialisation of Anglo-American Capitalism', *New Political Economy* 9:4, 539–58.

Lawson, Tony (1996) *Economics and Reality* (London: Routledge).

Lichtheim, George (1960) 'Review of the Constitution of Liberty', *Twentieth Century* (under the pseudonym of G. Arnold): 107.

McNeill, John (2001) *Something New Under the Sun: An Environmental History of the World in the Twentieth Century* (London: Penguin).

Mandel, Ernest (1978) *Late Capitalism* (London: Verso).

Marx, Karl (1976) *Capital* Vol. 1 (London: Penguin).

Meredith, Robyn (2008) *The Elephant and the Dragon* (New York: Norton).

Minsky, Hyman (2008) *John Maynard Keynes* (New York: McGraw-Hill).

Monbiot, George (2003) *The Age of Consent: A Manifesto for a New World Order* (London: Flamingo).

Monbiot, George (2006) *Heat: How to Stop the Planet Burning* (London: Allen Lane).

Moran, Michael (1990) *The Politics of the Financial Services Revolution: The USA, the UK, and Japan* (Basingstoke and New York: Palgrave Macmillan).

Moran, Michael (2003) *The British Regulatory State: High Modernism and Hyper-innovation* (Oxford: Oxford University Press).

Morris, Charles (2008) *The Trillion Dollar Meltdown* (New York: Public Affairs).

Narlikar, Amrita (2005) *The World Trade Organisation* (Oxford: Oxford University Press).

Noel, Alan and Jean Philippe Thèrien (2008) *Left and Right in Global Politics* (Cambridge: Cambridge University Press).

Nye, Joseph (2002) *The Paradox of American Power* (New York: Oxford University Press).

Ohmae, Kenichi (1995) *The End of the Nation-state* (London: HarperCollins).

Payne, Anthony (2005) *The Global Politics of Unequal Development* (Basingstoke and New York: Palgrave Macmillan).

Peston, Robert (2008) *Who Runs Britain?* (London: Hodder & Stoughton).

Pierson, Paul (1994) *Dismantling the Welfare State? Reagan, Thatcher and the Politics of Retrenchment* (Cambridge: Cambridge University Press).

Polanyi, Karl (2001) *The Great Transformation: The Political and Economic Origins of Our Time* (Boston: Beacon Books).

Rapkin, David (2005) 'Empire and its Discontents', *New Political Economy* 10:3, 389–412.

Rauchway, Eric (2008) *The Great Depression and the New Deal* (Oxford: Oxford University Press).

Robison, Richard (ed.) (2006) *The Neo-Liberal Revolution: Forging the Market State* (Basingstoke and New York: Palgrave Macmillan).

Rosamond, Ben (2000) *Theories of European Integration* (Basingstoke and New York: Palgrave Macmillan).

Rosenberg, Justin (2005) 'Globalization Theory: A Postmortem', *International Politics* 42:1, 2–74.

Rupert, Mark (2005) 'Reflections on Some Lessons Learned from a Decade of Globalization Studies', *New Political Economy* 10:4, 457–78.

Ryner, Magnus and Alan Cafruny (2007) *Europe at Bay: In the Shadow of US Hegemony* (Boulder, CO: Lynne Rienner).

Sassoon, Donald (1996) *One Hundred Years of Socialism: The West European Left in the Twentieth Century* (London: Tauris).

Schmidt, Vivien (2002) *The Futures of European Capitalism* (Oxford: Oxford University Press).

Scholte, Jan Aart (2005) *Globalisation* (Basingstoke and New York: Palgrave Macmillan).

Schumpeter, Joseph (1976) *Capitalism, Socialism and Democracy* (London: Routledge).

Schwartz, Herman (2000) *States versus Markets: The Emergence of a Global Economy* (Basingstoke and New York: Palgrave Macmillan).

Schwartz, Herman and Leonard Seabrooke (eds) (2008) Special Issue: The Political Cost of Property Booms, *Comparative European Politics* 6:3.

Seabrooke, Leonard (2007) 'Everyday Legitimacy and International Financial Orders: The Social Sources of Imperialism and Hegemony in Global Finance', *New Political Economy* 12:1, 1–18.

Seldon, Anthony (2007) *Blair Unbound* (London: Simon & Schuster).

Shonfield, Andrew (1965) *Modern Capitalism* (Oxford: Oxford University Press).

Sinclair, Tim (2005) *The New Masters of Capital: American Bond Rating Agencies and the Politics of Creditworthiness* (Ithaca, NY: Cornell University Press).

Skidelsky, Robert (1983) *John Maynard Keynes:1 Hopes Betrayed 1883–1920* (London: Macmillan).

Skidelsky, Robert (1992) *John Maynard Keynes: 2 The Economist as Saviour 1920–1937* (London:Macmillan).

Skidelsky, Robert (2000) *John Maynard Keynes: 3 Fighting for Britain 1937–1946* (London: Macmillan).

Soros, George (2008) *The New Paradigm for Financial Markets: The Credit Crisis of 2008 and What it Means* (London: Public Affairs).

Stelzer, Irwin (2005) *Neoconservatism* (New York: Atlantic Books).

Stewart, Michael (1986) *Keynes and After* (London: Penguin).

Stiglitz, Joseph (2002) *Globalization and its Discontents* (London: Allen Lane).

Strange, Susan (1986) *Casino Capitalism* (Oxford: Basil Blackwell).

Strange, Susan (1998) *Mad Money* (Manchester: Manchester University Press).

Swedberg, Richard (1991) *Joseph Schumpeter: His Life and Work* (Cambridge: Polity).

Sweezy, Paul (1968) *The Theory of Capitalist Development: Principles of Marxian Political Theory* (New York: Monthly Review Press).

Temin, Peter (1976) *Did Monetary Forces Cause the Great Depression?* (New York: Norton).

Thirkell-White, Ben (2007) 'The International Financial Architecture and the Limits to Neo-liberal Hegemony', *New Political Economy* 12:1, 19–42.

Thompson, Helen (2008) *Might, Right, Prosperity and Consent: Representative Democracy and the International Economy 1919–2001* (Manchester: Manchester University Press).

Turner, Rachel (2008) *Neo-liberal Ideology: History, Concepts and Policies* (Edinburgh: Edinburgh University Press).

Wade, Robert (2007) 'A New Financial Architecture?', *New Left Review* 46, 113–29.

Wade, Robert (2008) 'Financial Regime Change' *New Left Review* 53, 5–22.

Wolf, Martin (2005) *Why Globalization Works* (New Haven, CT: Yale University Press).

Wyss, David (2007) 'The Subprime Market: Housing and Debt', *Standard and Poor's Research*, 15 March.

Index